FLAUBERT AND JOYCE
THE RITE OF FICTION

1. The Orbit of Thomas Mann. By Erich Kahler

2. On Four Modern Humanists:
Hofmannsthal, Gundolf, Curtius, Kantorowicz.
Edited by Arthur R. Evans, Jr.

3. Flaubert and Joyce: The Rite of Fiction.
By Richard D. Cross

RICHARD K. CROSS

Flaubert and Joyce

THE RITE OF FICTION

PRINCETON UNIVERSITY PRESS

PRINCETON, NEW JERSEY

1971

Copyright © 1971 by Princeton University Press
ALL RIGHTS RESERVED
L.C. Card: 73-136197
I.S.B.N.: 0-691-06199-8
Publication of this book has been aided
by the Whitney Darrow Publication Reserve Fund
of Princeton University Press
This book has been composed in Linotype Primer
Printed in the United States of America
by Princeton University Press, Princeton, New Jersey

PREFACE

$\mathcal{T}$he novels of Flaubert and Joyce have not suffered any lack of scholarly attention. Surprisingly little has been done, though, to relate the two artists' achievements to each other, despite the fact that, as Frank Budgen recounts, "of all the great nineteenth century masters of fiction, Joyce held Flaubert in highest esteem," having read every line of his works and committed whole pages of them to memory.[1] I am not suggesting a need for *Quellenforschungen*; efforts to unravel the many strands of influence in an *oeuvre* as complex as Joyce's are likely to prove unproductive.

[1] *James Joyce and the Making of "Ulysses"* (Bloomington, Ind., 1960), pp. 179-180, 176. Budgen was Joyce's confidant during the wartime years both men spent in Zurich, and there is no reason to doubt the accuracy of his report.
Of the published criticism that deals specifically with the connection between Flaubert and Joyce, four items are significant: Ezra Pound's 1922 review of *Ulysses*, "James Joyce et Pécuchet," *Mercure de France*, CLVI, 307-320; Haskell M. Block, "Theory of Language in Gustave Flaubert and James Joyce," *Revue de Littérature Comparée*, XXXV (1961), 197-206; Hugh Kenner, *Flaubert, Joyce and Beckett: The Stoic Comedians* (Boston, 1962); and David Hayman, "*A Portrait of the Artist as a Young Man* and *L'Education Sentimentale*: The Structural Affinities," *Orbis Litterarum*, XIX (1964), 161-175. Harry Levin calls attention to parallels between Flaubert and Joyce's careers and attitudes toward art in a number of passages in his *James Joyce: A Critical Introduction*, rev. ed. (Norfolk, Conn., 1960), *Contexts of Criticism* (New York, 1963), and *The Gates of Horn* (New York, 1963), but, though his remarks are often suggestive, he does not treat the relationship between the two novelists in detail.

One may ask of even the most convincing source studies how much they illumine the artistic imagination and its works. "Far more important than the direct influence which Flaubert exerted on Joyce's thought and expression," Haskell Block rightly remarks, "is the pervasive affinity of mind and art which places both writers in a common literary tradition."[2]

If an artist's talent is genuine, the temper of his mind reveals itself most fully in his work. It follows that the best means of probing the kinship of the two novelists is to compare aspects of tone, theme, and technique in their writings. Flaubert challenged the historical criticism of Sainte-Beuve and Taine, demanding, "When will they be artists, nothing but artists, real artists? Where have you seen a criticism that is concerned, intensely concerned, with the work *in itself*? The milieu in which it was produced and the circumstances which occasioned it are very closely analyzed; but the unconscious poetics which are its source? Its composition? Its style? The author's point of view? Never!"[3] The hundred years since Flaubert raised these questions have seen the development of a variety of methods that do much to realize the critical program he proposed. Above all, the belief he shared with Joyce in the autonomy of art, which underlies his insistence on the centrality of "l'oeuvre *en soi*," has become a touchstone of modern criticism. My response to it in this study has been to keep the solid tissue of their fiction as clearly in view as possible: close textual analyses lie at the root of nearly all my comparisons of the two writers. Any consideration of the affinity between

---

[2] Block, p. 202.
[3] *The Selected Letters of Gustave Flaubert*, trans. and ed. Francis Steegmuller (New York, 1953), p. 218 (*Correspondance* [Paris: Conard, 1926-1933], VI, 8).

Flaubert and Joyce must, of course, take into account the cultural history of the two generations which separate their careers, but I have tried to keep this background material from becoming obtrusive.

The most effective way to compare the two bodies of fiction, it seemed to me, was to juxtapose in a given chapter elements of a single book by each artist. Naturally I wished to treat only works which had a significant bearing on each other. It proved possible to make such rapprochements in the case of all the full-length novels save *Salammbô*, a curious epic of Carthage in the grip of harsh gods, and *Finnegans Wake*, the even stranger night-epic of all times and races. In fact all of Flaubert's historical narratives except *La Tentation de saint Antoine* and, in a very limited way, *La Légende de saint Julien l'hospitalier* resist comparison with Joyce's work. The *Wake* is a *tour de force*. One may discover some precedent for Joyce's last book in the phantasmagoria of *Saint Antoine* or the encyclopedism of *Bouvard et Pécuchet*, but I preferred to treat these aspects of Flaubert's novels in conjunction with chapters of *Ulysses* where the parallels are closer. The chronology of Joyce's writings determined the order of the chapters of textual analysis, since his stylistic development is more nearly linear than Flaubert's and it seemed desirable to deal with the *Ulysses* episodes in their normal sequence.

"In an age of disbelief," remarked Wallace Stevens, "it is for the poet to supply the satisfactions of belief."[4] And since Flaubert and Joyce regularly celebrated the writer and his art in sacerdotal metaphors, the opening chapter discusses some of the special problems confronting them—the artist's isolation, the threats to his

[4] *Opus Posthumous*, ed. S. F. Morse (New York, 1957), p. 206.

integrity, the agony of composition—in terms of a priestly vocation. The concluding chapter attempts to define the core of the affinity between the two novelists in terms of their aesthetics and thus to draw together threads that run through the entire study. It seeks also to mark the limits of Joyce's sympathy with Flaubert.

I wish to thank Professors Albert J. Guerard, Robert G. Cohn, and Thomas C. Moser of Stanford, Professor A. Walton Litz of Princeton, and Professor Robert Martin Adams of the University of California, Los Angeles, who read various drafts of this work and offered much valuable advice and encouragement. Mrs. Eve Hanle, Mrs. Linda Peterson, and Miss Miriam Brokaw of the Princeton University Press made many helpful suggestions as it was in its final stages. I am also grateful to Stanford University, the University of California, and the Whitney Darrow Fund for grants which made its completion and publication possible.

Los Angeles   RICHARD K. CROSS
May 1970

ACKNOWLEDGMENTS

Quotations from the following works appear with the kind permission of the publishers:

From Gustave Flaubert, MADAME BOVARY, translated by Francis Steegmuller
Copyright © 1957 by Francis Steegmuller
Reprinted by permission of Random House, Inc.

From Gustave Flaubert, SENTIMENTAL EDUCATION, translated by Robert Baldick
Copyright © 1964 by Robert Baldick
Reprinted by permission of Penguin Books Ltd

From Gustave Flaubert, THREE TALES, translated by Robert Baldick
Copyright © 1961 by Robert Baldick
Reprinted by permission of Penguin Books Ltd

From Gustave Flaubert, BOUVARD AND PECUCHET, translated by T. W. Earp and G. W. Stonier
Copyright © 1954 by New Directions Publishing Corporation
Reprinted by permission of New Directions Publishing Corporation

From THE SELECTED LETTERS OF GUSTAVE FLAUBERT, translated and edited by Francis Steegmuller
Copyright © 1953 by Francis Steegmuller
Reprinted by permission of Farrar, Straus, and Giroux, Inc.

From DUBLINERS by James Joyce
Originally published by B. W. Huebsch in 1916
Copyright © 1967 by the Estate of James Joyce
All rights reserved
Reprinted by permission of The Viking Press, Inc., Jonathan Cape Ltd, and The Society of Authors as literary representative of the James Joyce Estate

From A PORTRAIT OF THE ARTIST AS A YOUNG MAN by James Joyce
Copyright 1916 by B. W. Huebsch, renewed 1944 by Nora Joyce
Copyright © 1964 by the Estate of James Joyce
All rights reserved
Reprinted by permission of The Viking Press, Inc., Jonathan Cape Ltd, and The Society of Authors

CONTENTS

PREFACE   v

ACKNOWLEDGMENTS   ix

I. THE PRIESTHOOD OF ART
Two Vocations   5

II. DEAD SELVES
Epiphanies in *Trois Contes* and
Dubliners   17

III. LES NOURRITURES CELESTES
Sympathy and Judgment in *L'Education
sentimentale* and *A Portrait of the Artist
as a Young Man*   35

IV. SEA CHANGES
The Rendering of Inward Experience in
Madame Bovary and *Proteus*   71

V. JEUNES FILLES EN FLEURS
Spatial Form in *Madame Bovary* and
Nausicaa   95

VI. THE NETHERMOST ABYSS
Expressionism in *La Tentation de saint
Antoine* and *Circe*   125

VII. IMPASSIVE STARS
The Vision of Fact in *Bouvard et
Pécuchet* and *Ithaca*   153

VIII. INVISIBLE NOVELISTS
The Core of the Affinity and Its Limits   177

INDEX   193

FLAUBERT AND JOYCE

THE RITE OF FICTION

I have just made a fresh copy of what I have
written since New Year, or rather since the
middle of February, for on my return from Paris
I burned all my January work. It amounts to
thirteen pages, no more, no less, thirteen pages
in seven weeks. However, they are in shape,
I think, and as perfect as I can make them.
There are only two or three repetitions of the
same word which must be removed, and
two turns of phrase that are still too
much alike.
—FLAUBERT, Letter to Louise Colet

I enquired about *Ulysses*. Was it progressing?
"I have been working hard on it all day," said Joyce.
"Does that mean you have written a great deal?" I said.
"Two sentences," said Joyce.
I looked sideways but Joyce was not smiling. I thought
    of Flaubert.
"You have been seeking the *mot juste*?" I said.
"No," said Joyce. "I have the words already.
    What I am seeking is the
    perfect order of words in the sentence."
—FRANK BUDGEN, *James Joyce
and the Making of "Ulysses"*

His true Penelope was Flaubert,
He fished by obstinate isles.
—EZRA POUND, "E. P. Ode pour
l'élection de son sépulcre"

CHAPTER I

THE PRIESTHOOD OF ART

TWO VOCATIONS

To readers who know Flaubert and Joyce best for their scrupulous portraits of burgher-life it seems natural to bracket the two writers as "realists." "Flaubert belongs to Rouen as Joyce belongs to Dublin," remarks Philip Spencer. "Essentially drab in spite of its cradle of woodland scenery and emphatically contemporary in spite of its medieval past," he goes on to say, "Rouen was synonymous with commerce and commerce at its most uninviting: a greyness of spirit seemed to droop over the river and seep into the hearts of the inhabitants."[1] One cannot help recalling the brown tints, emblematic of Dublin's moral paralysis, that Joyce deploys in his early stories. Sombre city-scapes are not, however, the final truth of either man's art, for both insisted on the poetry of inward experience as well as fidelity to naturalistic surfaces. Each of them carried within himself the germ of symbolism, which constituted a potent strain even in their early works and developed into the major mode of Joyce's later fiction.

Rouen serves as the locale of several episodes in *Madame Bovary*, but otherwise Flaubert made no direct artistic use of the city he knew so well. Paradoxically it

[1] *Flaubert* (New York, 1952), p. 13.

seems to have determined the attitudes that underlie his *oeuvre* to an even greater extent than was the case with Joyce's Dublin youth; Flaubert's moral and aesthetic views appear to have changed relatively little after his move to Croisset. His fascination with the grotesque began with his playing in the dissecting rooms of the Hôtel-Dieu, and it was there that he honed his powers of observation and analysis. "Son and brother of distinguished physicians," observed Saint-Beuve, "M. Gustave Flaubert holds the pen as others do the scalpel."[2] His hatred of bourgeois *moeurs*, many of which he continued to observe even as he exposed their vacuity in his novels, and his collection of *idées reçues* have their roots in Rouen as well. At age nine the future author of *Bouvard et Pécuchet* remarked in a letter to his schoolmate Ernest Chevalier, "And since there's a lady who comes to see papa and always says stupid things, I'll write them too."[3]

In spite of the fact that Joyce spent his adult life wandering from place to place on the Continent, the tie to his native city remains unmistakable. Like Odysseus coming home to his Penelope, Joyce returns to "dear, dirty Dublin" for the settings of all his books. To infer, though, that his imagination failed to enlarge itself during the years of exile would be to misjudge him seriously. Admitting the decisive character of youthful experience, a great many incidents drawn from the author's mature life found their way into the novels[4] and his moral vision deepened enormously. The

[2] *Causeries du lundi* (Paris, 1851-1862), XIII, 363 (my translation).

[3] *The Selected Letters of Gustave Flaubert*, trans. and ed. Francis Steegmuller (New York, 1953), p. 7 (*Correspondance* [Paris: Conard, 1926-1933] I, 1).

[4] A simple but representative instance of Joyce's transferring his European experiences to an Irish setting is the half-serious

main reason for transposing these impressions and insights to a Dublin setting lies, I believe, in Joyce's recognition that only in art could he recover his lost fatherland and redeem his pledge to draw Ireland more fully into the civilization of the West. If he was unable to forge a new conscience for his race, he could at least create a fresh image of it in the European mind. The Dubliners provided him also with one indispensable resource that Flaubert's Rouennais lacked, a vivacity of speech and gesture. Stephen Dedalus may have moments when he feels as though he is walking among "heaps of dead language,"[5] but his author managed to find verve even in his compatriots' clichés. Joyce's Liffey is not the counterpart of the miasmal Seine that flows through the opening pages of *L'Education sentimentale*; by the time we see it in *Finnegans Wake* the murky stream has come to represent the "hitherand-thithering waters" of life.

The battle of Romanticism, still being waged in the provinces during the 1830's, had an impact on Flaubert comparable to that of the Decadence of the nineties on Joyce. Both writers' apprentice fiction reveals minds given to expansive reveries, which offered escape from a materialism whose vulgarity at once appalled and intrigued them. Flaubert spoke of the opposing tendencies of his mind as "deux bonshommes distincts": "one who is infatuated with bombast, lyricism, eagle flights, sonorities of phrase and the high

---

liaison he conducted with Marthe Fleischmann in Zurich in 1918-1919. His dalliance corresponds in a number of details to Bloom's relationships with Gerty MacDowell and Martha Clifford (see Richard Ellmann, *James Joyce* [New York, 1959], pp. 462-467).

[5] *A Portrait of the Artist as a Young Man*, ed., Chester Anderson and Richard Ellmann (New York: Viking, 1964), p. 179.

points of ideas; and another who digs and burrows into the truth as deeply as he can, who likes to treat a humble fact as respectfully as a big one, who would like to make you feel almost *physically* the things he reproduces; this latter person likes to laugh, and enjoys the animal sides of man."[6] He tried unsuccessfully to effect an ironic fusion of the lyrical and the grotesque in the first *Education sentimentale* (1843-1845), and ten years later he accomplished it in such brilliant episodes of *Madame Bovary* as the agricultural fair and the rendezvous of Emma and Léon at the Rouen cathedral.

Joyce also struggled to reconcile conflicting impulses in his art. The protagonist of *Stephen Hero* refers to them as the classical and romantic "tempers." Possessed of "an insecure, unsatisfied, impatient temper," the romantic "sees no fit abode here for [his] ideals and chooses therefore to behold them under insensible figures . . . lacking the gravity of solid bodies." The classical temper, "ever mindful of limitations," draws strength from its focus upon "these present things" but finds itself forced to cope with "the materialism that must attend it."[7] Especially in *Ulysses*, Joyce mediates with consummate skill between the world of dreams and ideals on the one hand and that of everyday reality on the other. An extraordinary capacity for integration, for welding dissonant elements into artistic wholes, is in fact the primary attribute of Joyce's and Flaubert's brand of imagination. "Imagination" must be understood here as what Coleridge called the esemplastic

[6] *Selected Letters*, p. 127 (*Correspondance*, II, 343-344).

[7] *Stephen Hero*, ed. Theodore Spencer, John J. Slocum, and Herbert Cahoon (Norfolk, Conn., 1963), pp. 78-79. The split in sensibility to which Joyce's two tempers and Flaubert's "bonshommes distincts" refer corresponds in a general way to the stylistic breach between symbolism and naturalism.

power rather than in its popular sense of inventiveness in matters of plot and setting. Both artists reserve their creative energies for audacious technical experiments, and when it comes to form neither man repeats himself.

The two writers' preoccupation with style did not, of course, preclude a concern with the details of their subject matter. They were simply less inclined than most novelists to spend themselves fabricating material that could be more accurately drawn from observation. "The more Art develops," Flaubert believed, "the more scientific it will be" in the rigor of its methods.[8] Their conscientiousness as craftsmen led them to make even the most minute particulars the objects of painstaking research. An example of the French master's scrupulousness in authenticating details may be seen in a letter to Ernest Feydeau in which he requests information pertaining to *L'Education sentimentale*:

> This is what I should like to know—it concerns my book:
>
> My hero Frédéric quite properly wants to have a little more money in his pocket, and he plays the market. . . . This takes place in the summer of 1847.
>
> So: from May to the end of August, what were the securities favored by speculators?
>
> My story has three phases:
>
> 1. Frédéric goes to a broker with his money and follows the broker's advice. Is that how it's done?
> 2. He makes a profit. How? How much?
> 3. He loses everything. How? Why?
>
> It would be very good of you to send me this information—the episode shouldn't take up more

[8] *Selected Letters*, p. 132 (*Correspondance*, II, 395).

than six or seven lines in my book. But explain it all to me clearly and exactly.[9]

One need not look far to find a parallel instance of Joyce's fastidiousness. He frequently wrote to his aunt, Mrs. William Murray, to verify factual points concerning Dublin life. The following query, relating to an incident in the *Ithaca* chapter of *Ulysses*, is representative:

"Is it possible for an ordinary person to climb over the area railings of no 7 Eccles street, either from the path or the steps, lower himself down from the lowest part of the railing till his feet are within 2 feet or 3 of the ground and drop unhurt. I saw it done myself but by a man of rather athletic build. I require this information in detail in order to determine the wording of a paragraph."[10]

The two writers' obsession with literal fidelity to even the smallest facts exceeds the requirements of novelistic verisimilitude. Walton Litz cites Joyce's letter as evidence of his "desperate need for principles of order and authority. Deprived of social and religious order by his self-imposed exile, and acutely aware of the disintegrating forces in modern European society, Joyce turned to the concrete details of place and character as one stable base for his writing."[11] These observations apply almost equally to the internal émigré Flaubert, who sought refuge from his time in unremitting labor and an aesthetic mysticism that anticipates Joyce's priesthood of the imagination: "disgusted, frustrated, corrupted, and brutalized by the outside world . . . decent and sensitive people are forced to seek

[9] *Selected Letters*, p. 210 (*Correspondance*, v, 261-262).
[10] *Letters of James Joyce*, ed. Stuart Gilbert and Richard Ellmann (New York, 1957-1966), I, 175.
[11] *The Art of James Joyce* (London, 1961), p. 24.

somewhere within themselves a more suitable place to live. If society continues on its present path I think we shall see a return of such mystics as have existed in all the dark ages of the world."[12] Given this cast of mind, the attraction of Saints Anthony and Julian and his comparison of "les affres de l'Art" to an ascetic's hair-shirt are not hard to understand.

Finding it impossible to submit to any creed—"I believe that a thinker (and what is an artist if not a triple thinker?) should have neither religion, country, nor even any social convictions"—Flaubert knelt only before the altar of art, that least mendacious of lies.[13] Joyce reaffirms the need for detachment when he has Stephen decide to become a wildgoose and fly by the nets of church, nationality, and language. The Irish novelist sought to transcend not just the parochialism of the Gaelic revival but ultimately even the constraints of a usurper's tongue. In *Finnegans Wake* he aspires to a pan-European idiom, although, as anyone who has read passages aloud can testify, his fundamental medium remains a Dublin-accented English. His sole commitment was to express himself as fully and as freely as he could and to avoid any form of engagement that might deflect his vision or representation of the truth.[14] Joyce's fear of oppressive institutions and attitudes led to his insistence that the writer isolate himself from any influence that threatened the purity of his vocation: "This radical principle of artistic economy applies specially to a time of crisis,"[15] he declared in 1901, and at no point during the forty critical years

[12] *Selected Letters*, pp. 140-141 (*Correspondance*, III, 16).
[13] *Selected Letters*, p. 151 (*Correspondance*, III, 183). "De tous les mensonges, c'est encore le moins menteur" (I, 232).
[14] Cf. *Portrait*, pp. 203, 247.
[15] *The Critical Writings of James Joyce*, ed. Ellsworth Mason and Richard Ellmann (New York, 1959), p. 69.

that ensued did he display the slightest readiness to compromise.

Flaubert, who felt that bourgeois society posed a grave menace to personal and artistic liberty, was even more adamant in asserting that the writer must "climb into his ivory tower" in order to keep faith with his calling.[16] His fierce independence made even the sort of family life that gave Joyce solace an impossibility. "For me, marriage would be an apostasy which it appalls me to think of," he told his mother. "If you are involved in life you see it badly; your sight is affected either by suffering or by enjoyment. The artist, in my way of thinking, is a monstrosity, something outside nature."[17]

In spite of their early and imperious vocations, neither novelist published any fiction until he was in his mid-thirties. Flaubert, who wrote chiefly for his own satisfaction and that of a few close friends, remained largely indifferent to the prospect of literary fame. His artistic conscience rendered unthinkable the idea of relinquishing control over a book in any measure less perfect than he felt he could make it. "It is very doubtful that the public will ever have occasion to read a single line written by me," he avowed in 1846; "if this happens, it will not be before ten years, at least."[18] Exactly a decade later he yielded to Maxime Du Camp's pleas and allowed the serialization of *Madame Bovary* in the *Revue de Paris*.

Flaubert's longanimity calls to mind Stephen Dedalus' claim, mocked by Mulligan, that he is "going to write something in ten years."[19] Joyce places at the end

---

[16] *Correspondance*, ıı, 396 (my translation).
[17] *Selected Letters*, pp. 112-113 (*Correspondance*, ıı, 268-269).
[18] *Selected Letters*, p. 63 (*Correspondance*, ı, 233).
[19] *Ulysses* (New York: Modern Library, 1961), p. 249.

of *A Portrait* the dates 1904-1914, as if to fulfill this promise, even though work on the book appears to have extended into 1915.[20] Unlike Flaubert, he was anxious to publish and eager for recognition, but a perusal of his letters to various editors reveals an artistic integrity every bit as unbending as the Frenchman's. His refusal to change or delete a relatively small number of passages in *Dubliners* delayed the book's publication for eight years, and his unwillingness to modify the *Portrait* in deference to conventional tastes led to its rejection by so many firms that he was very nearly obliged to have it printed privately.[21] *Ulysses* appeared only through the good offices of Sylvia Beach, whose Paris bookshop was for many years the sole place where copies of "his usylessly unreadable Blue Book of Eccles"[22] could be obtained, since, like *Madame Bovary*, it had incurred the disfavor of censors.

Add to the shortsightedness of publishers and critics and harassment by legal authorities such cares as near-blindness, poverty, a schizophrenic daughter, and the painstaking labor of composition and one begins to appreciate the stupefying cost of Joyce's vocation. What is more, the burden was not merely borne but borne with courage, patience, and humor. "I am now advised to go to Aix-les-Bains," he wrote to Harriet Weaver, "but am in Ithaca instead. I write and revise and correct with one or two eyes about twelve hours a day I should say, stopping for intervals of five minutes or so when I can't see anymore. My brain reels after it but that is nothing compared with the reeling of my reader's brain.

[20] Ellmann, *James Joyce*, p. 365.
[21] See Joyce's correspondence with publishers, especially Grant Richards, for the years 1906-1916 in *Letters*, I and II, *passim*. These letters are studded with the proud Flaubertian term "artist."
[22] *Finnegans Wake* (New York, 1959), p. 179.

CHAPTER II

DEAD SELVES

EPIPHANIES IN *TROIS CONTES* AND *DUBLINERS*

Julien parcourut de cette manière une plaine
interminable, puis des monticules de sable, et
enfin il se trouva sur un plateau dominant un
grand espace de pays. Des pierres plates étaient
clairsemées entre des caveaux en ruines.
On trébuchait sur des ossements de morts; de
place en place, des croix vermoulues se
penchaient d'un air lamentable. . . . Alors
son âme s'affaissa de honte.[1]

—La Légende de saint Julien l'hospitalier

Yes, the newspapers were right: snow was general
all over Ireland. It was falling on every part
of the dark central plain, on the treeless hills.
. . . It was falling, too, upon every part
of the lonely churchyard on the hill where
Michael Furey lay buried. It lay thickly
drifted on the crooked crosses and headstones,
on the spears of the little gate, on the barren
thorns. His soul swooned slowly as he
heard the snow falling faintly through the
universe. . . .

—"The Dead"

Except a corn of wheat fall into the ground
and die, it abideth alone: but if it die,
it bringeth forth much fruit.

*—*John 12:24

CHAPTER II

DEAD SELVES

EPIPHANIES IN *TROIS CONTES*

AND *DUBLINERS*

The reputations of Flaubert and Joyce do not depend upon their contributions to the short story, yet at a crucial point in his career each man distinguished himself in the genre. *Un Coeur simple* and "The Dead" are undisputed masterpieces, and *La Légende de saint Julien* and several of the other *Dubliners* stories stand near that mark. From the moment of publication *Trois Contes* enjoyed a critical esteem that Joyce's stories received initially only from the most discriminating readers, among them Ezra Pound, who observed that in *Dubliners* "English prose catches up with Flaubert."[2]

Any attempt to make rapprochements between the

1 "In this way Julian crossed an endless plain and then some sand-hills, and finally found himself on a plateau dominating a great stretch of country. Flat stones were strewn about among ruined burial vaults. He kept stumbling over dead men's bones; here and there worm-eaten crosses leaned over in a pitiful way. . . . Then his soul was overcome with shame." (*Three Tales*, trans. Robert Baldick [Harmondsworth: Penguin, 1961], p. 76. All translated passages are from this edition.)

2 "Past History," *The English Journal*, xxii (May, 1933), 351.

two collections must take into account the place of each work in its author's canon. Critics often regard Flaubert's tales as pendants to his novels, even though they diverge considerably in tone. *Madame Bovary* and *Un Coeur simple* share a Norman setting, but the disparity between their heroines' responses to it could hardly be greater. Félicité, the protagonist of the *conte*, inevitably reminds us of Catherine Leroux, the mute, inglorious farm worker who serves as a foil to Emma in the *Comices agricoles* chapter of the novel, and indeed we may think of *Un Coeur simple* as a counter-statement to *Madame Bovary*. Of all Flaubert's writings it is the one whose irony is least truculent, the one in which he allows his *tendresse* fullest expression: "I want to move sensitive souls to pity, to make them cry, being one myself,"[3] he wrote to Mme Roger des Genettes. The *conte* represents an extraordinary triumph of artistic economy, encompassing as it does a whole life within a mere sixty pages. Pound asserted that it embodies "all that anyone knows about writing."[4] *Un Coeur simple* and, to a lesser extent, its two companion pieces represent also a victory of the artist's ripe maturity over the despair and spiritual exhaustion of his last years, a time when financial worries, the death of his mother and many of his friends, and the composition of *Bouvard et Pécuchet* oppressed him.

Flaubert's novels reveal him as a more astringent critic of contemporary life than was Joyce. Certainly the Frenchman seems less inclined to create characters who arouse much sympathy in his readers. In the case of *Dubliners* and the *Trois Contes*, however, the

[3] *Correspondance* (Paris: Conard, 1926-1933), VII, 307 (my translation).

[4] *The Letters of Ezra Pound*, ed. D. O. Paige (New York, 1950), p. 89.

normal positions of the two artists are reversed, and one may attribute Joyce's relatively greater intransigence here at least partly to his being a very young writer. As S. L. Goldberg points out, "It is not that the stories fail to imply the importance of courage, self-knowledge, fulfilment, freedom, or even the plainer domestic virtues; nor do they lack pity of a kind. But a comparison with Chekhov (or *Ulysses* for that matter) shows how little these values mean in *Dubliners*, how little it reveals what they might *be* in the actual experience of ordinary people, how complacent is its superior viewpoint."[5] Goldberg's reservations seem to me just, if one makes a clear exception, as he does, of "The Dead," which Joyce wrote three years after leaving Dublin. The perspective of exile enabled him to strike a fairer balance between his compatriots' strengths and shortcomings. "Sometimes thinking of Ireland it seems to me that I have been unnecessarily harsh," he wrote his brother Stanislaus in September 1906. "I have not reproduced its ingenuous insularity and its hospitality. The latter 'virtue' so far as I can see does not exist elsewhere in Europe."[6]

To say that Joyce's stories are inferior to some of Chekhov's—or Flaubert's—is not, of course, to deny that they are impressive technically. The virtuosity with which Joyce splices naturalistic narrative and symbolic strands in "Clay" seems to me to place it among the better pieces in *Dubliners*, and its subject matter makes comparison with *Un Coeur simple* natural. Both tales concern themselves with the fate of humble and inno-

---

[5] *James Joyce* (New York, 1962), p. 39.

[6] *Letters of James Joyce*, ed. Stuart Gilbert and Richard Ellmann (New York, 1957-1966), II, 166. Ellmann believes that in having Gabriel Conroy remark on Irish hospitality in his after-dinner speech Joyce was "beginning the task of making amends" (*James Joyce* [New York, 1959], p. 254).

cent spinsters of the servant class whose impulse to love is repeatedly thwarted.

Flaubert and Joyce begin their stories with brief sketches of their protagonists that read as though they were ironic replies to Villiers de l'Isle-Adam's *bon mot,* "Vivre? les serviteurs feront cela pour nous."[7] These passages are worth quoting in part as examples of the writers' exceptional dexterity in presenting exposition:

> Pendant un demi-siècle, les bourgeoises de Pont-l'Evêque envièrent à Mme Aubain sa servante Félicité. . . .
>
> Elle se levait dès l'aube, pour ne pas manquer la messe, et travaillait jusqu'au soir sans interruption. . . . Quant à la propreté, le poli de ses casseroles faisait le désespoir des autres servantes. Econome, elle mangeait avec lenteur, et recueillait du doigt sur la table les miettes de son pain,— un pain de douze livres, cuit exprès pour elle, et qui durait vingt jours. . . .
>
> Son visage était maigre et sa voix aiguë. A vingt-cinq ans, on lui en donnait quarante. Dès la cinquantaine, elle ne marqua plus aucun âge;—et, toujours silencieuse, la taille droite et les gestes mesurés, semblait une femme en bois, fonctionnait d'une manière automatique.[8]

[7] *Axël* (Paris, 1912), p. 287: "As for living, our servants will do that for us."

[8] *Trois Contes* (Paris: Conard, 1910), pp. 3-6. Subsequent page references will appear in parentheses in the text.

"For half a century the women of Pont-l'Evêque envied Mme Aubain her maidservant Félicité. . . .

"Every day Félicité got up at dawn, so as not to miss Mass, and worked until evening without stopping. . . . As for cleanliness, the shine on her saucepans was the despair of all the other servants. Being of a thrifty nature, she ate slowly, picking up the crumbs from her loaf of bread—a twelve-pound loaf

The matron had given her leave to go out as soon as the women's tea was over and Maria looked forward to her evening out. The kitchen was spick and span: the cook said you could see yourself in the big copper boilers. The fire was nice and bright and on one of the side-tables were four very big barmbracks. . . . Maria had cut them herself.

Maria was a very, very small person indeed but she had a very long nose and a very long chin. She talked a little through her nose, always soothingly: *Yes, my dear*, and *No, my dear*. She was always sent for when the women quarrelled over their tubs and always succeeded in making peace. One day the matron had said to her:

—Maria, you are a veritable peace-maker!

And the sub-matron and two of the Board ladies had heard the compliment. . . . Everyone was so fond of Maria.[9]

Flaubert, offering the reader a panoramic view of Félicité, fixes her Norman peasant character firmly in its milieu. Her piety, simplicity, industry, and capacity for endurance are rendered evident by a few vivid details. She is indeed the steadfast "femme en bois," as her deliberateness in picking up the crumbs on the table indicates. The nun-like discipline and fidelity re-

---

which was baked specially for her and lasted her twenty days. . . .

"Her face was thin and her voice was sharp. At twenty-five she was often taken for forty; once she reached fifty, she stopped looking any age in particular. Always silent and upright and deliberate in her movements, she looked like a wooden doll driven by clock-work" (17-18).

[9] *Dubliners*, ed. Robert Scholes (New York: Viking, 1967), p. 99. Subsequent page references will be incorporated in the text.

vealed in Félicité's bearing elicit our respect for her
calling. As Pound has observed, the thematic fulcrum
on which the *Trois Contes* balance is stated in the middle of *Saint Julien*: "et l'idée lui vint d'employer son
existence au service des autres" (118).[10] The essence of
sainthood for the skeptic Flaubert resides in the sanc-
tity of a servitude informed by love.

In *Un Coeur simple* the author endows the commonplace with immense significance, anticipating Joyce's
art of the epiphany. "When the relation of the parts is
exquisite, when the parts are adjusted to a special
point," declares Joyce's protagonist in *Stephen Hero*,
"we recognize that it is *that* thing which it is. Its soul,
its whatness, leaps to us from the vestment of appearance. The soul of the commonest object, the structure
of which is so adjusted, seems to us radiant."[11] The
religious overtones of the term "epiphany" make it as
appropriate a metaphor for the symbolic realism of
Trois Contes as it is for that of *Dubliners*.

Flaubert concludes his story by having Félicité, *in*

[10] "And he was struck by the thought of spending his life in
the service of others" (82). Cf. Ezra Pound, "James Joyce et
Pécuchet," *Mercure de France*, CLVI (June 1, 1922), 308.

[11] *Stephen Hero*, ed. Theodore Spencer, John J. Slocum, and
Herbert Cahoon (Norfolk, Conn., 1963), p. 213. Exactly what
Joyce meant by "epiphany" continues to exercise aestheticians.
In particular the question of where the significance in an epiphany resides, whether it inheres in "the vulgarity of speech or
of gesture" (211) or is conferred by an act of imagination or
entails a bringing to completion of potential meaning by the
artist, remains moot. The passage I have quoted places the
emphasis on the "adjustments" the mind must make for the
object to become luminous and, hence, on the artist's manipulation of his medium. I see no important distinction between
the process of epiphanization and that of symbol formation,
but in spite of its imprecision the term "epiphany" deserves to
be retained because it underscores the priestly character of the
writer's role.

extremis, confound a stuffed parrot with the Holy Spirit: "Les mouvements de son coeur se ralentirent un à un, plus vagues chaque fois, plus doux, comme une fontaine s'épuise, comme un écho disparaît; et, quand elle exhala son dernier souffle, elle crut voir, dans les cieux entr'ouverts, un perroquet gigantesque, planant au-dessus de sa tête" (63-64).[12] The disposition of elements in this sentence and their interruption, the impeded rhythm that corresponds to the slackening of her breath and pulse, lend great dignity to suffering that might easily have appeared nothing more than absurd. One may compare its effect, a sense of personal identity bleeding out into the cosmos, to the spectral cadences that close "The Dead."

Speaking of Félicité's epiphany, Flaubert avowed that it was "not at all ironic . . . but on the contrary very serious and very sad."[13] From the opening lines of the *conte* he has prepared the reader to respond with sympathy, if not to the apotheosis of Loulou, then at least to the condition of spirit which leads to her confusing parrot and Paraclete. Among the elements which contribute most directly to the effectiveness of the epiphany is the way he establishes her innocence, the simplicity and goodness of heart which enable her to love those familiar aspects of life which have been sanctified by God's dwelling among them: "elle aima plus tendrement les agneaux par l'amour de l'Agneau, les colombes à cause du Saint-Esprit" (24).[14] Félicité has diffi-

---

[12] "Her heart-beats grew slower and slower, each a little fainter and gentler, like a fountain running dry, an echo fading away. And as she breathed her last, she thought she could see, in the opening heavens, a gigantic parrot hovering above her head" (56).

[13] *Correspondance,* vii, 307 (my translation).

[14] "She loved the lambs more tenderly for love of the Lamb of God, and the doves for the sake of the Holy Ghost" (30).

culty in imagining the precise countenance of the Holy
Ghost, which is described in the Gospels as a bird, a
fire, and a breath, until she notices in a stained glass
portrait of the third Person a resemblance to her parrot. Before long she is saying her prayers in front of
Loulou, and her last act is the sacrifice of the stuffed
bird, her dearest possession, for use in adorning a Cor-
pus Christi altar. Flaubert adroitly anticipates the form
of her beatific vision in a hallucination on the water-
front at Honfleur in which, after tripping over a haw-
ser, she sees horses being lowered through a hatch:
"puis le terrain s'abaissa, des lumières s'entre-croi-
sèrent, et elle se crut folle, en apercevant des chevaux
dans le ciel" (29).[15] No schematic treatment can do
justice to the subtle adjustment of these parts to a focal
point at which the soul "leaps to us from the vestment
of appearance" in all its effulgence. Blessed are the
pure in heart, for they shall see God in an incarnation
they can comprehend. Flaubert's epiphany reveals an
astonishing imaginative daring.

Critics, many of whom find Flaubert's handling of
the characters in his novels excessively severe, are
often embarrassed by the peculiar shape his tenderness
assumes in *Un Coeur simple*. They recall that his writing of *Trois Contes* constituted a parenthesis in his
work on *Bouvard et Pécuchet* and that the latter book
was consecrated to a massive assault on the confusion
of words and values. Harry Levin speaks for those dis-
turbed by Loulou's translation: "Is the divine afflatus
to be identified with the chattering squawk of repeti-
tious mimicry? Has the Logos of civilization been ad-
dled by its own cult of Loulou: a mindless parroting of

---

[15] "Then the ground fell away, rays of light crisscrossed in
front of her, and for a moment she thought she was going mad,
for she could see horses up in the sky" (33).

words, a meaningless re-echoing of sounds, a gigantic case of psittacism? No one can ever have labored more strenuously than Flaubert to validate the Word."[16]

The parrot's reiteration of the three phrases Félicité has taught him is in fact a parody of cliché. Furthermore the residents of Pont-l'Evêque make the bird himself a subject of cant.[17] The artist suspends his satiric irony only on his heroine's behalf, and he does so by lending his own eloquence to her inarticulate pathos. Indeed at one point in the narrative his identification with her becomes virtually complete. She has been struck down at the same spot on the Honfleur road where Flaubert suffered his initial attack of epilepsy, and the ensuing moment of recognition so alien to her barely developed consciousness seems much more nearly *his* epiphany:

"Arrivée au sommet d'Ecquemauville, elle aperçut les lumières de Honfleur qui scintillaient dans la nuit comme une quantité d'étoiles; la mer, plus loin, s'étalait confusément. Alors une faiblesse l'arrêta; et la misère de son enfance, la déception du premier amour, le départ de son neveu, la mort de Virginie, comme les flots d'une marée, revinrent à la fois, et lui montant à la gorge, l'étouffaient." (51)[18]

If Flaubert's charity toward Félicité is uncharac-

---

[16] *The Gates of Horn* (New York, 1963), p. 293.

[17] Cf. the excellent discussion of the satiric dimension of the *conte* in Victor Brombert, *The Novels of Flaubert* (Princeton, 1966), pp. 240-241.

[18] "As she reached the top of the hill at Ecquemauville, she saw the lights of Honfleur twinkling in the darkness like a host of stars, and the shadowy expanse of the sea beyond. Then a sudden feeling of faintness made her stop; and the misery of her childhood, the disappointment of her first love, the departure of her nephew, and the death of Virginie all came back to her at once like the waves of a rising tide, and, welling up in her throat, choked her" (48).

teristic, Joyce's treatment of Maria conforms perfectly
to the embittered vision of decay and futility central
to *Dubliners*. In the opening passage previously quoted,
Joyce presents his exposition in the guise of a dramatic
scene, employing the idiom and speech rhythms of the
characters themselves. He allows adjectives in particular to depict, and to imply an evaluation of, Maria.
Writing from her point of view in the first paragraph,
he uses pairs of descriptive terms—"spick and span,"
"nice and bright"—which are formulas of convention-
alized perception. The rhetoric imitates exactly the cast
of mind of a simple laundry worker who seeks to mag-
nify in importance the trivial incidents which fill her
day: "These barmbracks seemed uncut; but if you
went closer you would see that they had been cut into
long thick even slices and were ready to be handed
round at tea. Maria had cut them herself" (99).

Joyce maintains the same propriety in the second
paragraph, which offers a general description of his
heroine. The folk trait of repeating words for emphasis—"Maria was a very, very small person but she had
a very long nose and a very long chin"—serves not only
to furnish us with details of her physiognomy but also
suggests that she is in some way witchlike. Joyce notes
several times that when she laughs the tip of her nose
almost meets her chin. The Dublin by Lamplight
laundry in which she is employed has as its stated
purpose "recovery from the Devil's dominance."[19] Her
name, the epithet "peace-maker," Joe's calling her his
"proper mother," and the curious veneration she is
said to receive from her fellow workers imply a resemblance to the Virgin Mary. The story takes place on the
last day of October and was initially entitled "Hallow
Eve." Marvin Magalaner and Richard Kain believe that

[19] Don Gifford, *Notes for Joyce* (New York, 1967), p. 53.

the church holiday provides a key to the symbolic relationship between hag and Virgin: "the day set aside in honor of saints . . . has had its eve perverted by celebrants to the calling forth of witches."[20] Speculations of this sort remain tenuous, since Joyce does not establish the kind of firm dramatic base for these overtones that Flaubert does for Félicité's identification of Loulou with the Holy Ghost but rather leaves them at the level of subdued implication. It seems evident, at any rate, that the counterpointing of Maria's attributes is designed to call attention to the displacement of traditional values. In the world of *Dubliners* perpetual virginity signifies barrenness rather than redeeming innocence. We are told that Maria is a peacemaker, but when she tries to reconcile Joe and Alphy, the boys she has reared, she proves to be pitifully ineffectual.

The witch and the Virgin indicate the limits of Maria's plight, which is developed much more fully in terms of naturalistic narrative. As in *Un Coeur simple*, the epiphany has its main roots in this soil, scrupulously tilled by the artist. He plants the qualities of vanity and self-deception essential to its flowering in the first paragraph of the story and skillfully cultivates them in the pages that follow. Circumstances have obliged his heroine to seek her livelihood, like Zola's Gervaise, in a laundry, and she tries to put the best face on the matter she can. Joe and Alphy have been kind enough, she rationalizes, to get her a "position" in an institution to whose "genteel" matron she feels closer than she does to a "common woman" like Mooney, who actually spends her days over the tubs. Not only does Maria claim a superior refinement, but she has not genuinely resigned herself to lifelong spin-

[20] *Joyce: The Man, the Work, the Reputation* (New York, 1962), p. 100.

sterhood, although the reader and all the other characters in "Clay" know that she has no real alternative.
Her manifest plainness notwithstanding, she is capable of mild conceit about her appearance: "she looked
with quaint affection at the diminutive body which she
had so often adorned. In spite of its years she found
it a nice tidy little body" (101). The courtesy of "the
colonel looking gentleman" on the Drumcondra tram
so disconcerts her that she forgets the plum cake she
had selected with such difficulty. Joyce adumbrates the
divination game at the Donnellys in the banter of the
laundresses over her picking the ring, the emblem of
marriage: "Maria had to laugh and say she didn't want
any ring or man either; and when she laughed her
grey-green eyes sparkled with disappointed shyness"
(101).

One can hardly blame poor Maria for clinging to
these illusions. Although she is barely more self-aware
than Félicité, she lacks the latter's capacity for loving
without expectation of requital and the delusions are
her only means of preserving the shred of *amour
propre* she needs to endure a hopelessly drab life. Most
commentators assume that she remains oblivious to
the truth of her situation even when it comes into
clearest focus during the divination game and the singing of "I Dreamt that I Dwelt." Certainly the illumination is most vivid for the reader, but it seems to me
that Joyce hints at a faint recognition on Maria's part
of her death-in-life. When her hand descends, to her
hosts' discomfiture, on the saucer of clay, the symbol
of mortality, she understands "that it was wrong that
time" (105). And she appears to accept Mrs. Donnelly's
judgment that the prayerbook she gets on the second
try indicates that her destiny lies in conventual isolation. She cannot, of course, relinquish all her yearn-

ings, but she renders the tune from Balfe's *Bohemian Girl* affirming impossible cravings for riches, rank, beauty, and love "in a tiny quavering voice" (106) and, perhaps not wholly unconsciously, she omits a stanza expressing the most implausible hope, that of marriage. The pathos of this occurrence leaves Joe "very much moved . . . and his eyes filled up so much with tears that he could not find what he was looking for and in the end he had to ask his wife to tell him where the corkscrew was" (106).

Joyce allows Joe to engage in this awkward attempt to conceal emotion that completes his own and Maria's exposure in a manner that does not compromise the author's ironic objectivity. In his determination not to elicit a sentimental response from his reader, however, the artist has, I believe, lapsed into gratuitous cruelty. One longs for a measure of the compassion Flaubert grants to Félicité or Baudelaire to his *petites vieilles*:

Ils trottent, tout pareils à des marionettes;
Se traînent, comme font les animaux blessés,
Ou dansent, sans vouloir danser, pauvres sonnettes
Où se pend un Démon sans pitié![21]

The mortality motif that runs through Joyce's stories culminates in the celebrated epiphany of Gabriel Conroy, the point at which *Dubliners* approaches most nearly the sacrificial vision of *Trois Contes*. Readers who approach "The Dead" from the perspective of the preceding fourteen stories tend to see Gabriel's vision as a revelation that he is, like the boy in "Araby," no more than "a creature driven and derided by vanity"

---

[21] "Les petites vieilles," *Oeuvres complètes* (Paris, 1961), p. 85: "They trot along like puppets, or hobble like lame animals, or, though they don't intend to, they do a kind of jig, like puny bells swung by a merciless demon" (*Baudelaire*, trans. and ed. Francis Scarfe [Baltimore, 1961], p. 196).

(35) or, like Mr. Duffy in "A Painful Case," an "outcast from life's feast" (117). Joyce's deployment of what appear to be deliberately ambivalent symbols[22] makes this line of interpretation plausible, but to my mind critics who follow it slight elements in the novella which indicate that he is groping his way toward the phoenix theme of *Finnegans Wake*. Unlike the protagonists of most of the later stories in *Dubliners*, Gabriel is wholly conscious of the significance of his epiphany. The glimpse he catches in the cheval-glass of his "well-filled shirt-front" (218) and his wife Gretta's disclosure of her nostalgia for her youthful beau engender in him "a shameful consciousness of his own person. . . . He saw himself as a ludicrous figure, acting as a penny-boy for his aunts, a nervous well-meaning sentimentalist, orating to vulgarians and idealising his own clownish lusts" (219-220).

Were his illumination to arrest itself at this stage he would differ in no important respect from James Duffy or the narrator of "Araby." Instead Joyce's hero resists the impulse to self-pity and confronts the threat to his worth as a man with courage, intelligence, and humility: "A vague terror seized Gabriel. . . . But he shook himself free of it with an effort of reason and continued to caress her hand" (220). In his tenderness toward Gretta, "his strange friendly pity for her" (222) and "generous tears," one may find the key to a modestly affirmative reading of "The Dead." Gabriel's charity extends even to Michael Furey. The feeling of oneness with his rival enables him to transcend narrow egoism and enter into communion with "all the living

22 Cf. Florence L. Walzl's perceptive consideration of the ambiguities of Gabriel's epiphany in "Gabriel and Michael: The Conclusion of 'The Dead,'" *James Joyce Quarterly* (fall, 1966), reprinted in James Joyce, *Dubliners*, ed. Robert Scholes and A. Walton Litz (New York, 1969), pp. 423-443.

and the dead" (224). Thus the fading out of his identity into the "grey impalpable world" (223) of the
shades need not entail irredeemable dissolution, for
the death of his old self implies the potentiality of
rebirth into a more authentic life. Joyce is moving
toward Leopold Bloom's awareness that "the touch of
a deadhand cures."[23]

Flaubert's narrative of the legendary Saint Julien,
rendered as a traditional fable, stands at a great distance from the technical *verismo* of the three stories
we have been considering, yet it is much closer than
one might suppose to the moral realism of *Un Coeur
simple* and "The Dead." Operating poetically within the
postulates of medieval faith, the artist presents us with
his most emphatic affirmation of the chances for self-
overcoming and spiritual liberation. The saint's illumination begins with a sense of impotence. He has
thrust his lance at a mad bull and seen it shatter: "Elle
éclata, comme si l'animal eût été de bronze. . . . Alors
son âme s'affaissa de honte. Un pouvoir supérieur
détruisait sa force" (108).[24] Julien's shame reveals to
him much less about the nature of his baseness than
does Gabriel's vision. Only in the abomination of par-
ricide and subsequent isolation from his kind can he
recognize the vanity of his own and other lives: "Le
besoin de se mêler à l'existence des autres le faisait
descendre dans la ville. Mais l'air bestial des figures,
le tapage des métiers, l'indifférence des propos glaç-
aient son coeur" (116).[25]

<hr/>

[23] *Ulysses* (New York: Modern Library, 1961), p. 514.

[24] "The lance was shivered to pieces, as if the animal were
made of bronze. . . . Then his soul was overcome with shame.
. . . Some higher power was rendering his strength ineffective"
(76).

[25] "The craving to take part in the life of other men impelled
him to go down into the city. But the bestial faces of the people

The need Julien feels to mingle his life with others, even with the fowls and beasts he had so avidly hunted, eventually finds its proper expression in the decision to serve them. Through loving sacrifices he rescues himself from despair and opens his soul to the possibility of redemption. The saint stretches out atop a leper to communicate the warmth of his body to the dying one in a spirit of utter self-abnegation: "Cependant une abondance de délices, une joie surhumaine descendait comme une inondation dans l'âme de Julien pâmé; et celui dont les bras le serraient toujours grandissait, grandissait, touchant de sa tête et de ses pieds les deux murs de la cabane. Le toit s'envola, le firmament se déployait;—et Julien monta vers les espaces bleus, face à face avec Notre-Seigneur Jésus, qui l'emportait dans le ciel" (124-125).[26] Like Gabriel Conroy, Saint Julien must lose his life in order to find it. Flaubert and Joyce are not writers given to facile yea-saying. The wisdom they grasped is concisely formulated in Saint Augustine's sentence—a favorite of Samuel Beckett's—concerning the two thieves crucified with Christ: "Do not despair; one of the thieves was saved. Do not presume; one of the thieves was damned."[27]

---

he met, the noise of their work, and the triviality of their conversation froze his heart" (81).

[26] "Meanwhile an abundance of delight, a superhuman joy swept like a flood into Julien's soul as he lay there in a swoon. And the one whose arms still held him tight grew and grew, until his head and his feet touched the walls of the hut. The roof blew off, the heavens unfolded—and Julian rose towards the blue, face to face with Our Lord Jesus Christ, who bore him up to heaven" (86-87).

[27] Quoted in Casebook on "Waiting for Godot," ed. Ruby Cohn (New York, 1967), p. 51. Cf. Beckett, Waiting for Godot (New York, 1954), p. 9f.

CHAPTER III

LES NOURRITURES CELESTES

SYMPATHY AND JUDGMENT
IN *L'EDUCATION SENTIMENTALE*
AND *A PORTRAIT OF THE ARTIST
AS A YOUNG MAN*

Se dió a entender que no le faltaba
otra cosa sino buscar una dama
de quien enamorarse: porque el
caballero andante sin amores era
árbol sin hojas y sin fruto y
cuerpo sin alma.[1]
                    —*Don Quixote*

Dans son ciel poétique resplendissait
un visage de femme, si bien qu'en la
voyant pour la première fois, il
l'avait reconnue.[2]
                    —*L'Education sentimentale*

He wanted to meet in the real world
the unsubstantial image which his
soul so constantly beheld.
                    —*A Portrait of the Artist*

CHAPTER III

LES NOURRITURES CELESTES

SYMPATHY AND JUDGMENT

IN *L'EDUCATION SENTIMENTALE*

AND *A PORTRAIT OF THE ARTIST*

AS A YOUNG MAN

*I*n our time one commonly assumes that a novelist's first book will be an essay in self-definition. Flaubert found it possible to complete *L'Education sentimentale*, however, only after he had perfected his fictional craft in *Madame Bovary* and *Salammbô*, and Joyce had to subject his talent to the discipline of *Dubliners* before he could cast *A Portrait of the Artist* in its proper mode. The two writers invested a great deal of their youthful experience in their *Bildungsromane*, but in neither of them do we find the sort of

[1] "He . . . found but one thing lacking still: he must seek out a lady of whom he could become enamored; for a knight-errant without a lady-love was like a tree without leaves or fruit, a body without a soul" (Miguel de Cervantes Saavedra, *Don Quixote*, trans. Samuel Putnam [New York, 1958], p. 29).

[2] "A woman's face used to shine in his poetic paradise, so that, the first time he had seen her, he had promptly recognized her." (*Sentimental Education*, trans. Robert Baldick [Baltimore: Penquin, 1964], p. 270. All translated passages are from this edition.)

formless self-indulgence characteristic of many auto-biographical novels. Both men did in fact produce juvenilia to which that description applies, but, as a matter of artistic conscience, they suppressed these early writings.[3] The final versions of the *Education* and the *Portrait* are the achievements of mature writers, capable of viewing their earlier lives with ironic detachment and not scrupling to diverge sharply from biographical fact when their fictive art demanded it. Flaubert and Joyce sought to depict representative young men, and to that end they refined aesthetically incongruous elements of their personalities and histories out of the narratives. (The essential appeal of autobiography for the artist is, after all, the opportunity not merely to write his life but to *re*-write it.)

Ultimately the two novels are significantly autobiographical as all works of art are autobiographical—in terms of the distinctive vision they embody. Defining the limits of authorial impersonality, Paul Bourget remarks rightly that "each of us perceives not the universe, not naked reality, but what his temperament permits him to appropriate from that reality. We relate only our dream of human life: every work of imagination is an autobiography, if not in a strictly material sense, at least in the sense of being intimately and profoundly indicative of the substrata of our nature."[4]

---

[3] Flaubert's *Mémoires d'un fou* (1838), *Novembre* (1843), and the first *Education sentimentale* (1845) all deal with material included in the *Education* of 1869, although it is completely recast in this last work. Joyce's *Stephen Hero* (1906) is readily recognizable as part of an early draft of the *Portrait*, but here again it differs markedly from the final version in tone and form. None of these immature efforts appeared in print during their authors' lifetimes; their subsequent publication was a convenience for scholars rather than a recognition of intrinsic merit.

[4] "Gustave Flaubert," *Essais de psychologie contemporaine* (Paris, 1901), I, 130 (my translation).

As a corollary of Bourget's observation, one may note that each reader's peculiar angle of vision colors his understanding of a given book and that, paradoxically, this coloration frequently assumes a deeper hue in more or less direct proportion to the degree of impersonality attained by the author. Often readers unwittingly take advantage of the absence of explicit rhetorical guidance in a work of fiction to inject their private views into the text. In the case of a novel whose vision is as intricate as that of *A Portrait of the Artist* or *L'Education sentimentale*, the problem of interpretation becomes exceptionally acute. Honest and intelligent readers of the former work in particular differ so sharply in their analyses of its meaning that they scarcely seem to be discussing the same book.[5]

Bildungsromane have as a characteristic theme the clash of youthful dreams and ideals with a disappointing reality. These two novels concern themselves particularly with the disparity between the protagonists' erotic and vocational aspirations and their success in

[5] The most penetrating discussion of the general question of artistic control in the novel is probably Wayne Booth's *Rhetoric of Fiction* (Chicago, 1961). Booth considers the special problems of the *Portrait* on pp. 323-336.

For a sample of opposing positions on Joyce's attitude toward Stephen Dedalus, see, on the one hand, Hugh Kenner, *Dublin's Joyce* (London, 1955), pp. 109-134, and Caroline Gordon, "Some Readings and Misreadings," *Sewanee Review*, LXI (1953), 388-393, and, on the other, W. Y. Tindall, *James Joyce: His Way of Interpreting the Modern World* (New York, 1950), *passim*, and Eugene M. Waith, "The Calling of Stephen Dedalus," *College English*, XVIII (1957), 256-261.

The question of what tone Flaubert adopts in his portrayal of Frédéric Moreau has engendered no comparable confusion, although some critics have argued over the precise nature of Frédéric's *éducation* or even whether any worthy of the name occurs: see, e.g., Jean-Pierre Richard, *Littérature et sensation* (Paris, 1954), pp. 181ff., and Martin Turnell, *The Novel in France* (New York, 1958), pp. 289-309.

realizing them. One of the more effective means of unraveling the complexities of tone is to compare the ways Flaubert and Joyce employ scenes that dramatize these dreams and disenchantments to bring their narratives into focus. Love and work become, then, the coordinates of our sympathy for and judgment of the principal characters.

The opening scene of the *Education* prefigures with great precision the central development of the novel, Frédéric Moreau's realization that he can never have the only woman he finds it possible to love.[6] The kernel of his sentimental education consists, as Jean-Pierre Richard points out, in his acceptance of that fact.[7] Flaubert paints a backdrop for Frédéric's initial encounter with Mme Arnoux that is characterized by an economy lacking in the work as a whole. We first see Frédéric standing on the deck of the river steamer *Ville de Montereau*, watching Paris disappear as the banks of the Seine "filèrent comme deux larges rubans que l'on déroule."[8] This figure, which recurs in various forms at a number of points in the book, suggests the unrolling of time, at once languid and inexorable, in which Frédéric is caught up and carried along.

The travelers aboard the boat do not constitute a very savory slice of humanity. Most of them are capable of no aspiration more profound than attaining pro-

[6] David Hayman, "*A Portrait of the Artist as a Young Man* and *L'Education sentimentale*: The Structural Affinities," *Orbis Litterarum*, xix (1964), 166-169, comments perceptively on the similarities between Frédéric's initial vision of Mme Arnoux and Stephen's wading girl epiphany.

[7] *Littérature et sensation*, p. 182.

[8] *L'Education sentimentale: histoire d'un jeune homme* (Paris: Conard, 1910), p. 2. Subsequent page references will appear in parentheses in the text. "The two banks . . . slipped past like two wide ribbons being unwound" (15).

prietorship of one of the "coquettes résidences" that line the river. Frédéric is, by contrast, the soul of ambition, or rather he is at least ambitious in his dreams. He thinks about the plot of a play, subjects for pictures, future loves. Flaubert makes it clear, though, that his hero does not strive to attain his desires, but passively attends the stroke of fate that will fulfill them. At eighteen he has already begun to bemoan his ill-luck: "Il trouvait que le bonheur mérité par l'excellence de son âme tardait à venir" (3).[9] The circumstances of Frédéric's voyage reveal just how dependent he is. Mme Moreau has sent him to see an uncle whose fortune she hopes will be left to her son. Since she has given him just enough money for the journey, he takes his spineless revenge for not being able to stay in Paris by returning home the longest way. One may infer that the mother-son relation substantially determines the shape of those "passions futures" on which he muses.

The squalid river boat seems the least likely setting in which to realize any of Frédéric's hopes. Thus, when he finally does encounter Mme Arnoux, the contrast heightens the effect, which takes on the intensity of a religious vision, "une apparition." We witness the transformation of a simple *bourgeoise* into a creature of celestial grace, possessed of dazzling eyes, radiant skin, delicate, translucent fingers, and fine features, etched against a backdrop of blue sky. In short, we find ourselves confronted with a Fra Angelico Madonna; only the babe is missing and within half a page she does in fact take her child on her lap. Mme Arnoux is nothing if not maternal. Not at all coincidentally, her Christian name is Marie. Only years later does Frédéric dare to

[9] "He considered that the happiness which his nobility of soul deserved was slow in coming" (16).

use it, "adorant ce nom-là, fait exprès, disait-il, pour
être soupiré dans l'extase, et qui semblait contenir des
nuages d'encens, des jonchées de roses" (391).[10] Even
as he stands on the deck of the boat his desire for physical possession of her gives way to a deeper yearning.
Flaubert assures us that it is not Frédéric's vanity
which leads him to give alms to the harpist who has
played for them but an impulse of the heart "presque
religieux."

The images of Mariolatry which frame Frédéric's
vision are not entirely congruent with his character,
as they would be for Stephen Dedalus, since it is nowhere shown that he has had any specifically Christian
experience. In this respect he differs not only from
Flaubert's hero-saints but also from Félicité in *Un
Coeur simple*, who is saintly in her own fashion, and
even Emma Bovary, who emphatically is not. The
source of these metaphors is rather the religion of
love which had attached itself to the romanticism prevalent in the 1830's, the period of Frédéric's adolescence.

"I do not know what schoolboys dream about now,"
Flaubert reflects in his preface to Louis Bouilhet's *Dernières Chansons*, "but our dreams were superb in their
extravagance. The last expanding developments of
romanticism, reaching us and being cramped and
squeezed in a provincial atmosphere, produced curious
effervescences in our brains. . . . We were not only
troubadours, insurrectionists and Orientals; we were,
above all else, artists."[11] In the second chapter of the
Education, we learn that Frédéric had once aspired to

[10] "He called her Marie, worshipping that name, which he
said was made specially to be breathed in ecstasy, and which
seemed to contain clouds of incense and trails of roses" (271).

[11] Preface to *Dernières Chansons*, 2nd ed. (Paris, 1874), pp.
7-8, trans. and quoted in Raymond Giraud, *The Unheroic Hero*
(New Brunswick, N.J., 1957), p. 135.

be the Walter Scott of France and that in literature he now prizes passion above all else: Werther, René, Franck, Lara, Lélia, and other more mediocre characters rouse him to indiscriminate enthusiasm. He has even composed verses, which his friend Deslauriers finds "fort beaux," without asking to see any others. Frédéric's sentiments are, then, representative of his generation as Flaubert conceives it.

Thus when Frédéric encounters Mme Arnoux, the profound attraction she exerts on him stems from the fact that, in his eyes, she resembles the heroines of romantic novels. Her dark complexion leads him to suppose that she is of Andalusian origin or, since she is attended by a Negress, a Creole. He imagines her wrapped in the shawl he sees draped over the rail of the *Ville de Montereau* on a ship in mid-ocean. This yearning for the exotic, which he associates with the erotic, finds expression in the bohemian harpist's song, "une romance orientale, où il était question de poignards, de fleurs et d'étoiles"; to Frédéric it seems like the "plainte d'un amour orgueilleux et vaincu" (8).[12] Flaubert undercuts the heavy sentimentality of this passage by noting that the boat's throbbing engine accompanies the melody "à fausse mesure."

It is at once poignant and intensely ironic that Mme Arnoux, when she does come to requite Frédéric's love, thinks of him in terms of the same romantic conventions that inform his image of her. At their last meeting she tells him:

"—Quelquefois, vos paroles me reviennent comme un écho lointain, comme le son d'une cloche apporté par le vent; et il me semble que vous êtes là, quand je lis des passages d'amour dans les livres.

[12] "It was an eastern romance, all about daggers, flowers, and stars . . . the sad story of a proud, unhappy love" (19).

"—Tout ce qu'on y blâme d'exagéré, vous me l'avez fait ressentir, dit Frédéric. Je comprends Werther que ne dégoûtent pas les tartines de Charlotte. (603)"[13]

Mme Arnoux's motives are never fully revealed to us, since we see her almost entirely from Frédéric's point of view.[14] For some readers, most notably Henry James, this mode of presentation constitutes a serious flaw in the novel: "Madame Arnoux is of course ever so much the best thing in [Frédéric's] life—which is saying little; but his life is made up of such queer material that we find ourselves displeased at her being 'in' it on whatever terms; all the more that she seems scarcely to affect, improve, or determine it."[15]

It would be pointless to tackle directly James's basic premise that Frédéric is an inadequate reflector; one suspects that it is, ultimately, a matter of taste which cannot be disputed. But the question he raises about the effect of Mme Arnoux does seem pertinent. Why is it that Frédéric's great dream, the dream which cen-

---

[13] " 'Sometimes your words come back to me like a distant echo, like the sound of a bell carried by the wind; and when I read about love in a book, I feel that you are there beside me.'
" 'You have made me feel all the things in books which people criticize as exaggerated,' said Frédéric. 'I can understand Werther not being put off by Charlotte's bread and butter' " (413).

[14] Emile Gérard-Gailly made an intriguing discovery that may at least in part account for the reluctance of Elisa Schlésinger, the model for Mme Arnoux, to consummate her liaison with Flaubert, viz., she was not legally Maurice Schlésinger's wife when Flaubert first met her in Trouville. Schlésinger had rescued her from an unhappy marriage with Emile-Jacques Judée (he had literally bought her), and a mixture of fear and gratitude seems to have constrained her to remain faithful to Schlésinger. Ironically, Flaubert could not have been aware of these facts. Cf. Gérard-Gailly, *Le grand amour de Flaubert* (Paris, 1944), chap. IV.

[15] *The Future of the Novel*, ed. Leon Edel (New York, 1956), p. 143.

ters on her, never comes within reach of realization? Some of the difficulties are evident in the first chapter. For one thing Frédéric, unlike Emma Bovary, is timid and requires encouragement; Mme Arnoux's reticence does not permit her to offer any. External circumstances, too, play a part in frustrating his hopes. When, after years of cultivation, he has broken through her impassiveness and appears to be on the point of eliciting the response he seeks, her child develops croup and, in gratitude for its deliverance, she sacrifices her love for Frédéric. The primary obstacle to the fulfillment of the dream lies, though, in the very nature of his desire. What is only implicit in the opening scene, when he feels an abyss opening between himself and Mme Arnoux, becomes overt when he tears up the love letter he has written, immobilized by a fear much deeper than the mere wish to avoid disappointment or humiliation. The sentiments of reverence and self-abasement which lie at the heart of Frédéric's romantic piety manifest themselves in the beatification of Mme Arnoux:

"L'action, pour certains hommes, est d'autant plus impraticable que le désir est plus fort. . . . Une invincible pudeur l'en empêchait; et il ne pouvait se guider d'après aucun exemple, puisque celle-là différait des autres. *Par la force de ses rêves,* il l'avait posée *en dehors des conditions humaines.* Il se sentait, à coté d'elle, moins important sur la terre que les brindilles de soie s'échappant de ses ciseaux." (245, my italics)[16]

In dreams begin Frédéric's responsibilities to Mme

[16] "For some men, the stronger the desire, the more difficult it is for them to act. . . . An invincible sense of decency restrained him; and he could not find any example to follow, since she was different from other women. His dreams had raised her to a position outside the human condition. Beside her, he felt less important on earth than the scraps of silk which fell from her scissors" (174).

Arnoux. His dreams give rise to desire and, at the same time, forbid him to gratify it: "Il voulait qu'elle se donnât, et non la prendre" (392).[17] Since she attracts him in large part because of her motherliness, it seems plain that the "invincible pudeur" which constrains him is the incest taboo. Far from scarcely seeming to affect or determine Frédéric's life, as James contends, his vision of Marie Arnoux governs the crucial aspects of his conduct—both his actions and his inaction. James's doubts about whether she "improves" his life are essentially irrelevant. What truly matters is, as Victor Brombert remarks, "the tragic urge to create such a figure, to believe in her, and to cling stubbornly to the beauty of a vision engendered, as it were, by the very banality of existence."[18]

A very large portion of Stephen Dedalus' sentimental education also consists of dreams in which he seeks

[17] "He wanted her to give herself, and not to take her" (272).

The best psychological explanation of the combination of desire and inhibition we see in Frédéric is to be found in Freud's celebrated essay on "The Most Prevalent Form of Degradation in Erotic Life," *Collected Papers of Sigmund Freud* (New York, 1959), IV, 203-216.

[18] *The Novels of Flaubert* (Princeton, 1966), p. 145. Professor Brombert provides a suggestive discussion of the whole first chapter of the *Education*, joining it with the brothel scene at the end of the book (cf. especially pp. 140-146).

One must be careful about linking the term "tragic" with Frédéric. Edmund Wilson suggests, it seems to me, the sense in which it may be accurately applied to the *Education*: "It is the tragedy of nobody in particular, but of the human race itself reduced to such ineptitude, such cowardice, such commonness, such weak irresolution—arriving, with so many fine notions in its head, so many noble words on its lips, at a failure which is all the more miserable because those who have failed are hardly conscious of having done so" ("Flaubert's Politics," *The Triple Thinkers*, London, 1938, pp. 113-114).

refuge from "the dull phenomenon of Dublin."[19] There are, of course, important differences in the foci of the *Education* and the *Portrait*. The most obvious of these is the discrepancy in the ages of the two protagonists. The *Education* begins with Frédéric on the threshold of manhood, the suspended chord on which the *Portrait* ends. Frédéric is eighteen when he first sees Mme Arnoux and Stephen only a few years older when he leaves for Paris. We witness intimately the latter's development from the moment in infancy when he awakens to self-consciousness, whereas in the case of the former we have only occasional passages of exposition dealing with his adolescence and the concluding pages in which Frédéric and Deslauriers, now middle-aged, exhume their abortive youthful sally on Zoraïde Turc's bordello. The most radical phase of Frédéric's moral and emotional formation has been completed before the novel opens, and he seems, in comparison with Stephen, a static character. The forty-five-year-old man who, during the final rendezvous with Marie Arnoux, rejects what he suspects is her offer to consummate their love rather than degrade his ideal is fundamentally the same, except for an increased awareness of his own motives, as the youth who passively contemplated her on the deck of the steamer or even the boy who fled from the Turk's place. As they part for the last time, Mme Arnoux kisses him on the forehead "comme une mère" (606).

For many readers the variations on a common theme that stand in lieu of a conventional plot in the *Education* are not varied enough to keep a work of six hun-

---

[19] *A Portrait of the Artist as a Young Man*, ed. Chester G. Anderson and Richard Ellmann (New York: Viking, 1964), p. 78.

dred pages from becoming tedious. The *Portrait*, on the other hand, dramatically fuses a number of disparate themes that wind through Stephen's maturation and compresses them into less than half the space of Flaubert's novel. Erotic dreams and desires come to the fore in the second chapter of the *Portrait*, the point at which Stephen's pubescence is represented. Even more than in Frédéric's case, love is for Stephen essentially a matter of self-dramatization. "The female role in the *Portrait*," observes Hugh Kenner, "is less to arouse than to elucidate masculine desires."[20] If Frédéric constitutes Mme Arnoux in large measure out of the stuff of dreams, the women we see in the *Portrait* are to an even greater extent the shadowy issue of Stephen's reveries. None of them possesses anything like the permanence of Frédéric's vision.

Flaubert mentions in passing the characters in romantic fiction who have contributed their forms to Frédéric's ideals and expectations, but Joyce shows us this process in detail. Language has for Stephen a mystical potency: "Words which he did not understand he said over and over to himself till he had learned them by heart: and through them he had glimpses of the real world" (62). His way of preparing himself for a place in that reality was to immerse himself in *The Count of Monte Cristo*. The Dumas romance serves to launch his own imaginings, in which he, naturally, plays the part of the "dark avenger." Not just the parlor table on which he constructs a replica of Edmond Dantes's treasure cave but his whole environment undergoes a metamorphosis: "Outside Blackrock, on the road that led to the mountains, stood a small whitewashed house in the garden of which grew many rose-

[20] *Dublin's Joyce*, p. 129.

bushes: and in this house, he told himself, another Mercedes lived" (62-63). Mercedes is, of course, the heroine of Dumas' story, but Stephen extends her role to include many marvelous adventures of his own devising. The roses which grow in her garden (cf. Mme Arnoux's "jonchées de roses") belong to a key motif which is intertwined with the themes of sex, religion, and artistic creativity. The mythic overtones of the garden require no comment, except to note that this one harbors, as Marianne Moore's figure has it, real toads.

In the denouement of Stephen's imaginary adventures romantic fantasy doubles as prophecy:

"There appeared an image of himself, grown older and sadder, standing in a moonlit garden with Mercedes who had so many years before slighted his love, and with a sadly proud gesture of refusal, saying:

"—Madam, I never eat muscatel grapes." (63)

Mercedes serves here as a figure for the Church, and the "sadly proud gesture of refusal" adumbrates Stephen's defiant *non serviam*, his repudiation of the eucharistic grapes and a priestly vocation.

At this point in the novel the Dedaluses begin to suffer the effects of economic reverses which reinforce Stephen's growing unrest and sense of isolation. Rather than play with other children, he tries to find solace in brooding upon the image of Mercedes. But his dreaming only intensifies the turmoil in his heart and sends him roaming the neighborhood in a vague quest for satisfaction:

"He wanted to meet in the real world the unsubstantial image which his soul so constantly beheld. He did not know where to seek it or how: but a premonition which led him on told him that this image would, without any overt act of his, encounter him. They would

meet quietly as if they had known each other and had
made their tryst, perhaps at one of the gates or in some
more secret place. They would be alone, surrounded
by darkness and silence: and in that moment of su-
preme tenderness he would be transfigured. Weakness
and timidity and inexperience would fall from him in
that magic moment." (65)

These reflections look forward to the appearance of
a whole series of feminine figures ranging from a
Nighttown whore to the wading girl at the Bull Wall,
all of them seeming to promise the apotheosis he craves
and none of them actually providing it. Stephen's development depends instead on a gradual accumulation
of partial epiphanies.

Finally Simon Dedalus' debts compel the family to
move to Dublin; his son experiences the change of fortune as a "reshaping [of] the world about him into a
vision of squalor and insincerity" (67). Ironically, the
transfer enables Stephen to meet the first apparent incarnation of his feminine ideal. The circumstances are
analogous to the ones in which the meditation on the
"unsubstantial image" takes place. A children's party
is in progress and, like Frédéric on the deck of the river
steamer, Stephen feels isolated from his fellows. At this
moment he perceives the girl who is later identified as
Emma Clery and whose glance effects "a feverish agi-
tation of his blood" (68).

They leave the party together, she with her shawl
drawn around her head like a cowl. This trace of religious attire is significant, for Emma, like his vision-
ary Mercedes, comes to be closely associated with the
religion he feels compelled to deny. He is aroused by
her flirting and yet some scruple restrains him: "He
heard what her eyes said to him from beneath their
cowl and he knew that in some dim past, whether in

life or in revery, he had heard their tale before. He saw her urge her vanities, her fine dress and sash and long black stockings, and knew that he had yielded to them a thousand times. Yet a voice within him spoke above the noise of his dancing heart, asking him would he take her gift to which he had only to stretch out his hand." (69)

Ostensibly Stephen's temptation in this scene is simply sexual. But then he remembers the incident which has prefigured it—Eileen Vance's putting her cool white hand in his pocket and running with her fair hair streaming out behind her, the time when the liturgical phrases "Tower of Ivory" and "House of Gold" had acquired a distinctive meaning for him (42-43). This recollection gives him pause. It is not just timidity that keeps him from catching hold of Emma on the tram steps and kissing her, but, symbolically, a reluctance to entangle himself in the net she represents. Frédéric Moreau's inaction proceeds from a wish to avert the destruction of his ideal and Stephen's from a fear of embracing a false ideal which would destroy him. Much later, after he has openly spurned the Church, he accuses Emma of flirting with a priest, and not, unfortunately, with "the priest of eternal imagination" (221) he envisions himself to be.

Even at this comparatively early stage in his development, though, Stephen attempts to turn the encounter on the tram steps toward an aesthetic end. He writes a sentimental lyric in which the grosser elements of the experience—the tram, the tram-men, the horses—are refined away, just as the sordid milieu in which Frédéric first sees Mme Arnoux is suppressed in his vision of her. Stephen cannot, however, eliminate altogether the religious overtones of his relationship with Emma, even during the process of poetic composition:

"From force of habit he had written at the top of the first page the initial letters of the jesuit motto" (71), *ad majorem Dei gloriam.* He can no more expunge the marks of his Catholic education than could Joyce himself.

The author allows Emma's role as a figure for the Church to remain subdued and implicit in the incident considered above. In the third chapter, he renders the identification explicit. Stephen has lapsed into carnality and is suffering pangs of conscience as a consequence. One of the sins to which his lust has led him is the ravishing of Emma in his mind. At this point he conceives of her as his intercessor, a diminutive version of heaven's queen who reconciles him with an angry God, albeit only temporarily: "God and the Blessed Virgin were too far from him. . . . But he imagined that he stood near Emma in a wide land and, humbly and in tears, bent and kissed the elbow of her sleeve" (116).

Confronted with a Dublin whose squalor and hypocrisy offend him deeply, Stephen strives in a number of ways to introduce some sort of redeeming design into his personal life, "to build a breakwater of order and elegance against the sordid tide of life without him and to dam up . . . the powerful recurrence of the tides within him" (98). Another facet of this impulse to order is the persistent need he feels to ritualize experience: "In vague sacrificial or sacramental acts alone his will seemed drawn to go forth to encounter reality: and it was partly the absence of an appointed rite which had always constrained him to inaction whether he had allowed silence to cover his anger or pride or had suffered only an embrace he longed to give" (159). Indeed only in the poem "To E— C—", which his tram ride with Emma has inspired, can Stephen yield himself:

"the kiss, which had been withheld by one, was given by both" (71). But "suffered only an embrace he longed to give" suggests even more strongly his encounter with the prostitute at the end of Chapter II.

Alienated from his family and community and moving "among distorted images of the outer world" (99), Stephen returns to his dreams of Mercedes. The hope of a transfiguring tryst, a "holy encounter . . . at which weakness and timidity and inexperience were to fall from him," alternates with a potent strain of youthful lust. One evening in Nighttown the two strands of desire intertwine: "A trembling seized him and his eyes grew dim. The yellow gasflames arose before his troubled vision against the vapoury sky, burning as if before an altar. Before the doors and in the lighted halls groups were gathered arrayed as for some rite. He was in another world: he had awakened from the slumber of centuries" (100). The religious similes in this passage indicate that Stephen wishes to think of his impending sexual initiation as a ceremony, a mystical Celtic rite of passage. He does in fact experience a sense of transport and liberation: "Tears of joy and relief shone in his delighted eyes. . . . In her arms he felt that he had suddenly become strong and fearless and sure of himself" (101).

At the same time, Joyce severely qualifies the significance of Stephen's "swoon of sin." Far from being a priestess, the prostitute remains a tawdry creature. Juxtaposed with the florid prose in which Stephen's feelings are expressed is her flippant speech—"Good night, Willie dear!" she says when she accosts him and calls him "a little rascal." Stephen is no more aggressive in this scene than in the one in which he is tempted by Emma; despite the strength and courage and confidence he claims to have discovered, he cannot make his lips speak nor bend to kiss the whore. "The absence of an *appointed* rite" constrains him and renders the epiphany partial and unstable. He must assimilate a great deal more experience—more than he has even when the *Portrait* closes—before he can hope, as a priest of art, to consecrate events on the authority of his own imagination. At this juncture, the best he can manage is a "vague" sacramental act, an ersatz rite. All the same, it *does* enable him "to go forth to encounter reality."

Those critics who see Stephen as a mere aesthete incapable of ever becoming a serious artist deny that he actually encounters reality or, at any rate, discount the fruitfulness of the experience. S. L. Goldberg is right, I believe, in maintaining that "the sexual encounter, the now half-instinctive, half-deliberate act of surrender and discovery is part of his growth. Given his social and moral circumstances, it exacerbates the divisions between his body and his soul, but it also discovers another undeniable part of himself and of the world he inhabits."[21] In particular, what he learns of the senses permits him to perceive the repellent "chill" of life as a Jesuit and thus helps to determine his choice of an artistic vocation.

Flaubert depicts as a kind of ritual Frédéric's preparations for the assignation he plans with Mme Arnoux in part II, Chapter VI of the *Education*. Frédéric undertakes to make the furnished room he has retained a suitable setting for the long-awaited consummation of his great passion: "plus dévotement que ceux qui font des reposoirs, il changea les meubles de place, drapa lui-même les rideaux, mit des bruyères sur la cheminée, des violettes sur la commode; il aurait voulu paver

---

[21] *James Joyce* (New York, 1962), p. 54.

la chambre tout en or" (396).²² Ironically, Frédéric's
fussy display of erotic piety comes to nothing. Mme
Arnoux submerges it in a genuine act of religious devotion: interpreting her son's illness as a divine warning
not to persist in her love for Frédéric and desiring to
express gratitude for the boy's recovery, "elle offrit à
Dieu, comme un holocauste, le sacrifice de sa première
passion, de sa seule faiblesse" (405).²³ Frédéric,
"homme de toutes les faiblesses" (429), has violated
the conditions of his ideal by seeking to possess her.
He heaps coals on his head by entering into a liaison
with Rosanette Bron based chiefly on spite: "Alors, par
un raffinement de haine, pour mieux outrager en son
âme Mme Arnoux, il l'emmena jusqu'à l'hôtel de la rue
Tronchet, dans le logement préparé pour l'autre"
(407).²⁴

Actually Frédéric practices the type of transposition
evident in the episode just discussed all through *L'Education sentimentale.* As Stephen Dedalus derives temporary satisfaction from a demimondaine whose image
is overlaid with his dream ideal, so Frédéric employs
the varied attributes of the women in his life in a
contrapuntal fashion:

"La fréquentation de ces deux femmes faisait dans
sa vie comme deux musiques: l'une folâtre, emportée,
divertissante, l'autre grave et presque religieuse; et,

²² "More reverently than somebody decking out an altar of
repose, he moved the furniture about, hung the curtains himself, and put heather on the mantelpiece and violets on the
chest of drawers. He would have liked to pave the whole room
with gold" (275).
²³ "She offered God, as a sacrifice, her first love, her only
weakness" (281).
²⁴ "Then, as a refinement of hatred, in order to degrade
Madame Arnoux more completely in his mind, he took Rosanette to the house in the Rue Trouchet, and into the room prepared for the other woman" (283).

vibrant à la fois, elles augmentaient toujours, et peu
à peu se mêlaient; car, si Mme Arnoux venait à l'ef-
fleurer du doigt seulement, l'image de l'autre, tout de
suite, se présentait à son désir, parce qu'il avait, de ce
côté-là, une chance moins lointaine; et, dans la com-
pagnie de Rosanette, quand il lui arrivait d'avoir le
coeur ému, il se rappelait immédiatement son grand
amour." (207)[25]

The finely wrought "deux musiques" passage exem-
plifies one of its author's most significant contributions
to fictional technique, a more precise and subtle means
of rendering psychological processes than his predeces-
sors possessed. As Martin Turnell observes, "Flaubert's
insight into the association of ideas, the way in which
the character's emotions for different women crystallize into images which alternately blend and clash, reinforce and destroy one another, anticipates some of
Bergson's researches and points the way to Proust and
Joyce."[26]

In the instance of the furnished room on the Rue
Tronchet, Frédéric's substitution of *la Maréchale*[27] for

[25] "The company of these two women made as it were two
melodies in his life: the one playful, wild, amusing; the other
grave and almost religious. And the two melodies, sounding at
the same time, swelled continually and gradually intermingled;
for, if Madame Arnoux merely brushed him with her finger,
his desire immediately conjured up the image of the other
woman, since in her case his hopes were less remote; while if,
in Rosanette's company, his heart happened to be stirred, he
promptly remembered his great love" (149).

[26] *The Novel in France*, p. 294. Proust might well have denied
the debt. To him Flaubert's images seemed feeble and his
metaphors lacking in fineness. Cf. Marcel Proust, *Chroniques*
(Paris, 1927), p. 194.

[27] Rosanette Bron, *la Maréchale*, was largely inspired by
Mme Aglaé Sabatier, *la Présidente*, who was courted at various
times by Baudelaire, Gautier, and Flaubert himself. Baudelaire's relationship with her resembled that of Flaubert with

Mme Arnoux represents an inverted tribute to his ideal and is partially forgivable, especially since he is ignorant of the circumstances which have prevented Mme Arnoux from keeping the rendezvous. During the affair with Mme Dambreuse, however, he approaches a complete profanation of the ideal. He *uses* his love ("il se servit du vieil amour," 524) in an attempt to infiltrate aristocratic Paris. Society strikes the jaded young man as an amusing alternative to the course he has been following, but looking upon Mme Dambreuse's scrawny bosom he finally recognizes "ce qu'il s'était caché, la désillusion de ses sens." The horror is that, despite his perception of emotional atrophy, "il n'en feignait pas moins de grandes ardeurs; mais pour les ressentir, il lui fallait évoquer l'image de Rosanette ou de Mme Arnoux" (536).[28]

In the end, his disgust at the crassness of his engagement to Mme Dambreuse—"une spéculation un peu ignoble" (596)—and anger at her affront to Mme Arnoux lead him to break with her. The action restores luster to his tarnished dream and represents, perhaps, Frédéric's nearest approach to heroism. His *grand amour* is hardly a consistent source of ennoblement; at least in part it accounts for his cold-hearted and selfish treatment of Rosanette and Louise Roque. But if Frédéric immolates others on the altar of his ideal, he is at least willing to sacrifice himself there too.

Mme Schlésinger in its simultaneity of desire and the need to avoid gratifying that desire—a nineteenth-century variation on the convention of courtly love. Mme Sabatier proved more accessible, however, and hence the illusion less durable.

[28] "He admitted at that moment what he had refused to acknowledge until then—the disillusionment of the senses. This did not prevent him from simulating ardent passion; but in order to feel it, he had to summon up the image of Rosanette or Madame Arnoux" (369).

As I indicated in my analysis of the opening pages of the *Education*, Flaubert presents Frédéric as a young man whose head is full of projects but who lacks the discipline to execute them. His love for Mme Arnoux provides a powerful stimulus for these aspirations and on many occasions it also promises, in Frédéric's own view, to galvanize him into seriously pursuing a vocation. This sense strongly possesses him after he has left the first of many dinner parties at the Arnoux'. His reactions to that event parallel in many respects his initial vision of Marie Arnoux. There occurs the same annihilation of time and space. Flaubert objectifies Frédéric's feelings in an impressionistic city-scape, which begins with an echo of the "deux rubans" image in the opening scene:

"Les réverbères brillaient en deux lignes droites, indéfiniment, et de longues flammes rouges vacillaient dans la profondeur de l'eau. Elle était de couleur ardoise, tandis que le ciel, plus clair, semblait soutenu par les grandes masses d'ombre qui se levaient de chaque côté du fleuve. Des édifices, que l'on n'apercevait pas, faisaient des redoublements d'obscurité. Un brouillard lumineux flottait au delà, sur les toits; tous les bruits se fondaient en un seul bourdonnement; un vent léger soufflait." (71)[29]

The paragraph stands as a fine example of Flaubert's skill in evoking a mood through description which com-

---

[29] "The street-lamps shone in two straight lines, stretching away into the distance, and long red flames flickered in the depths of the water. The river was the colour of slate, while the sky, which was brighter, seemed to be supported by the huge masses of shadow that rose on each side of the river. Buildings which the eye could not distinguish intensified the darkness. Further away, a luminous haze floated over the rooftops; all the noises of the night melted into a single murmur; a light breeze was blowing" (60).

bines sonorous rhythms and exact images, a species of lyricism at which Joyce too excels. More important for our immediate purpose, however, is the way in which this passage prepares the reader to evaluate the ensuing moment in which Frédéric experiences his sense of calling. As many commentators have observed, passion in Flaubert's novels tends to translate itself into metaphors of fluidity. In this scene flickering, melting, indistinctness, shadows, and luminous haze compose Frédéric's vision and mirror the enervating surge of tenderness within him.

Frédéric's passion makes, then, for an instability in which no firm vocation can take root. When his sensuous impressions give way to a daemonic transport, he is exposed to an utterly devasting irony: "Une faculté extraordinaire, dont il ne savait pas l'objet, lui était venue. Il se demanda, sérieusement, s'il serait un grand peintre ou un grand poète; et il se décida pour la peinture, car les exigences de ce métier le rapprocheraient de Mme Arnoux. Il avait donc trouvé sa vocation! Le but de son existence était clair maintenant, et l'avenir infaillible" (71).[30] Flaubert terminates this chimera with Deslauriers' snores. The reader knows perfectly well, when Frédéric buys a box of paints and contracts with Pellerin for lessons, that his artistic aspirations will go the way of his earlier attempts at writing, his legal career, and his later ventures into business and politics.

His true profession consists, it would seem, in loving

[30] "He had been endowed with an extraordinary talent, the object of which he did not know. He asked himself in all seriousness whether he was to be a great painter or a great poet; and he decided in favour of painting, for the demands of this profession would bring him closer to Madame Arnoux. So he had found his vocation! The object of his existence was now clear, and there could be no doubt about the future" (61).

Mme Arnoux and in that alone. "Les autres s'évertuent pour la richesse, la célébrité, le pouvoir! Moi, je n'ai pas d'état," he tells her in one of the most poignant speeches in the novel. "Vous êtes mon occupation exclusive, toute ma fortune, le but, le centre de mon existence, de mes pensées" (387).[31] Despite the self-pity and the hyperbole, Frédéric's affirmation is essentially genuine, and, as I have suggested, what modicum of dignity he possesses derives from his faith in her as the touchstone of all he thinks and does.

Feminine ideals never play so central a role in the *Portrait*. They point beyond themselves to the forces which contend for Stephen's soul. As in the *Education*, the hero's encounter with a woman engenders in him a sense of artistic vocation. But where Frédéric's calling is plainly a matter of self-deception, the authenticity of Stephen's continues to perplex critics. The appearance of Stephen in *Ulysses* as a demoralized drifter and in *Stephen Hero* as a rather pretentious figure whom the author deflates on occasion with irony and direct criticism, although not in an entirely consistent manner, seems to many readers to cast doubt on the claims he makes for himself in the last two chapters of the *Portrait*. Joyce's avoidance of explicit commentary has exacerbated this problem.

Toward the end of Chapter IV, after he has refused the call to the priesthood, Stephen wanders along the strand trying to sort out his own motives. The phrase he uses to express his mood of spiritual liberation and harmonize it with his milieu is "a day of dappled seaborne clouds" (166). It is not, he thinks, the romantic associations of these words that attract him: "No, it

[31] "Others strain after wealth, fame, power. I have no profession; you are my exclusive occupation, my entire fortune, the aim and centre of my life and thoughts" (269).

was not their colours: it was the poise and balance of
the period itself." Stephen needs these qualities, exem-
plified by the Newman whom he acknowledges as his
master in prose if not in thought, more than he realizes.
Having rejected ecclesiastical discipline, he must find
another principle of order which will confer poise and
balance on his feelings. As the revery unfolds, though,
restraint and lucidity diminish and a mood of mystical
ecstasy takes hold of him. Joyce employs a polychro-
matic Pateresque style, punctuated by the cries of
schoolboys, to depict Stephen's rising emotions. Stephen
finds his classmates repellent and withdraws further
into reflections on his strange surname, which strikes
him as having prophetic overtones:

"Now, at the name of the fabulous artificer, he
seemed to hear the noise of dim waves and to see a
winged form flying above the waves and slowly climb-
ing the air. What did it mean? Was it a quaint device
opening a page of some medieval book of prophecies
and symbols, a hawklike man flying sunward above the
sea, a prophecy of the end he had been born to serve
and had been following through the mists of childhood
and boyhood, a symbol of the artist forging anew in
his workshop out of the sluggish matter of the earth
a new soaring impalpable imperishable being?" (169)

Stephen responds to the tremulous "call of life" af-
firmatively, which means, initially, taking off his shoes
and going wading. Up to this point in the book, water
has been an ambivalent symbol, more often than not
one of fear and disgust. On his way to the beach
Stephen still thinks of water as "infrahuman," but now
it becomes the emblem of a rebirth into creativity. Its
new positive significance is underscored by Stephen's
vision of yet another incarnation of his feminine ideal.

Perhaps "incarnation" is too strong a term, for the girl who stands "in mid-stream, alone and still, gazing out to sea" (171) hardly exists outside his consciousness. She offers a metaphorical invitation to the artistic flight he longs to undertake: "She seemed like one whom magic had changed into the likeness of a strange and beautiful seabird. . . . A wild angel had appeared to him, the angel of mortal youth and beauty, an envoy from the fair courts of life, to throw open before him in an instant of ecstasy the gates of all the ways of error and glory. On and on and on and on" (171-172)!

On and on, indeed! It is not surprising that many critics have taken this kind of empurpled prose, followed by the austere style of the fifth chapter, as an instance of romantic irony, a disclosure, as Mark Schorer says, of "the illusory nature of the whole ambition."[32] Hugh Kenner calls attention to the images of "irresponsible motion" in this section of the novel and declares that "this riot of feelings corresponds to no vocation definable in mature terms."[33] In this view, Stephen becomes almost the exact counterpart of Frédéric, as are Little Chandler and some of the other characters in *Dubliners*. The analogy might obtain if we were to limit consideration to the final pages of Chapter IV of the *Portrait* and such passages as the one in part I, Chapter IV of the *Education* discussed earlier. But the "romantic temper"[34] Stephen evinces in this scene is just one stage in the development of a very young man which continues through the long fifth

[32] "Technique as Discovery," *Hudson Review* (1948), reprinted in Robert Scholes, ed., *Approaches to the Novel* (San Francisco, 1961), p. 261.

[33] *Dublin's Joyce*, p. 132.

[34] Cf. the discussion of the classical and romantic "tempers" in *Stephen Hero*, ed. Theodore Spencer, John J. Slocum, and Herbert Cahoon, rev. ed. (Norfolk, Conn., 1963), p. 78.

chapter and is not yet concluded on the last page of the novel (nor even in its sequel, *Ulysses*).

We see Frédéric make a number of false starts all through his twenties and beyond, and recognize early in the book, perhaps too early, that his artistic aspirations are futile. It is not at all clear, though, that Joyce means to disparage Stephen's hopes. "There are significant echoes of earlier 'triumphs,'" concedes Goldberg, but he goes on to remark—correctly, I believe—that "once again there is knowledge discovered amid the delusions. To be an artist it is first necessary to realize that one wants to be an artist."[35] Joyce is too conscientious a realist, too faithful to life, to allow grace to descend on his hero in a solitary thunderbolt. Stephen must earn the right to practice his art by encountering reality, which includes treading in "the ways of error."

We witness a portion of this long process in Chapter v, in which Stephen sharpens his critical faculty with regard to both literature and his own experience and produces the first piece of writing that we are permitted to inspect, a villanelle. Whether the poem is to be taken "as a serious sign of Stephen's artistry, as a sign of his genuine but amusingly pretentious precocity, or as something else entirely"[36] is, Wayne Booth points out, one of the crucial tests in determining what attitude Joyce intends us to adopt toward his protagonist.

Stephen undertakes to compose the poem, an action occupying eight pages, following his dialogue on aesthetics with Lynch. That episode ends with a shower that forces him to take refuge on the porch of the national library, from which point he notices his old inamorata, Emma. He wonders, in terms that recall the

[35] *James Joyce*, p. 58.
[36] *The Rhetoric of Fiction*, p. 328.

passage about the wading girl, whether he has judged her too harshly: "If her life were a simple rosary of hours, her life simple and strange as a bird's life, gay in the morning, restless all day, tired at sundown? Her heart simple and wilful as a bird's heart" (216)? The next we see of him, after this speculation on whether he has not played the hawk to her dove, he is awakening from sleep "all dewy wet. . . . In a dream or a vision he had known the ecstasy of seraphic life" (217).

Ten years after the incident on the tram steps that occasioned his first poem, Emma has again inspired him to compose verse. In his ecstatic vision she loses her particular identity and undergoes assimilation into the feminine ideal, which in this instance assumes the aspect of a mythical virgin temptress. Like the Emma upon whom he has meditated a short time before, the temptress has a "strange wilful heart, strange that no man had known or would know, wilful from before the beginning of the world," and, as in *Measure for Measure*, that heart baits a trap used to catch other celestial creatures: "lured by that ardent roselike glow the choirs of the seraphim were falling from heaven" (217). Stephen's moment of inspiration is very much a matter of burning with Pater's "hard, gemlike flame": "The instant flashed forth like a point of light and now from cloud on cloud of vague circumstance confused form was veiling softly its afterglow. O! In the virgin womb of the imagination the word was made flesh" (217). "The prose rises in nervous excitement," Hugh Kenner remarks in connection with a similar passage in Chapter IV, "to beat again and again the tambours of a fin-de-siècle ecstasy."[37] Furthermore, Stephen's vision sends forth its "rays of rhyme" (218) in the shape of a villa-

[37] *Dublin's Joyce*, p. 131.

nelle, a characteristic form of the nineties. On this basis, he does indeed appear to be among the progeny of Swinburne, Wilde, and the Celtic Twilight.[38]

The rhythmic impetus of Stephen's dream carries him through three stanzas, then dies. Were he to abandon the poem when the lyric cry lapses, we might properly dismiss him as being, at least at this point, nothing more than a posturing aesthete. Instead he places the composition on a firmer foundation. He considers soberly his relationship with Emma, and, accordingly, the narrative style takes on the precision and mordancy which, says Levin, define "the sustaining tone" of *A Portrait*:[39]

"Rude brutal anger routed the last lingering instant of ecstasy from his soul. It broke up violently her fair image and flung the fragments on all sides. On all sides distorted reflections of her image started from his memory: the flower-girl in the ragged dress with damp coarse hair and a hoyden's face who had called herself his own girl and begged his handsel, the kitchengirl in the next house who sang over the clatter of her plates with the drawl of a country singer the first bars of *By Killarney's Lakes and Fells. . . .*" (220)

Emma's image gives off these reflections because at this moment she is not so much a projection of Stephen's idealized erotic longings as "a figure of the

[38] George L. Geckle, "Stephen Dedalus and W. B. Yeats: The Making of the Villanelle," *Modern Fiction Studies*, xv (1969), 87-96, argues that Stephen's lyric and the exposition surrounding it were strongly affected by several of Yeats's early poems and, more particularly, by his essay on "The Symbolism of Poetry."

[39] *James Joyce*, p. 50. Levin believes that "Joyce's own contribution to English prose is to provide a more fluid medium for refracting sensations and impressions through the author's mind—to facilitate the transition from photographic realism to esthetic impressionism" (p. 50).

womanhood of her country, a batlike soul waking to the consciousness of itself in darkness and secrecy and loneliness" (221). She represents the common life he finds so distasteful but which he must encounter repeatedly and ultimately deal with artistically. He moves toward that realization in this episode when he conceives of himself as "a priest of imagination, transmuting the daily bread of experience into the radiant body of everliving life" (221). The phrasing of his perception is of course grandiloquent—Stephen remains shot through with pretension—but the process of transubstantiation and incarnation he envisages is in fact the essential task of the religion of art. Even now his insight enables him to go on with the villanelle:

"The radiant image of the eucharist united again in an instant his bitter and despairing thoughts, their cries arising unbroken in a hymn of thanksgiving.

> *Our broken cries and mournful lays*
> *Rise in one eucharistic hymn.*
> *Are you not weary of ardent ways?*
>
> *While sacrificing hands upraise*
> *The chalice flowing to the brim,*
> *Tell no more of enchanted days*." (221)

Few readers can accept the poem at Stephen's own high valuation, although recently Robert Scholes has offered an elaborate exegesis and defense. Scholes's interpretation strikes me as over-ingenious and his praise excessive, but I am inclined to agree with his observation that, "despite his bitterness, Stephen comes, through the composition of the poem, to an understanding of [Emma's] innocence, an equilibrium, a stasis, in which his new understanding and pity balance his old desire and bitterness."[40] It is not by any means a complete or permanent resolution. In the diary entries at the end of *A Portrait*, which function as points in an ellipsis linking that novel with *Ulysses*, Stephen realizes that a great distance lies between himself and his goal: "Mother is putting my new secondhand clothes in order. She prays now, she says, that I may learn in my own life and away from home and friends what the heart is and what it feels. Amen. So be it" (252). Nevertheless, the villanelle, with its difficult rhyme scheme, does reveal that Stephen has achieved a certain proficiency in his craft and that he is capable of submitting his imagination and feelings to the discipline of literary form. Surely it is not necessary that he be a Keats or a Rimbaud for us to credit his promise.

Commentators have compared both Mme Arnoux and Emma to the Beatrice who leads Dante from purgatory into paradise.[41] The parallel holds to the extent that Frédéric and Stephen do call upon feminine figures to guide them toward an earthly redemption. The two young men desperately require ways of transcending the banality, squalor, and deceit that permeate their existence; perhaps even more they need a means of

[40] "Stephen Dedalus, Poet or Esthete?" *PMLA*, LXXIX (1964), 485.

[41] Regarding Frédéric's first vision of Mme Arnoux, Brombert comments that "all this, seen through Frédéric's eyes, and Flaubert's art, transmutes a woman into an apparition, and makes of her, in the midst of a nineteenth-century scene of everyday life, a sister to Beatrice.

> e par che sia una cosa venuta
> da cielo in terra a miracol mostrare." (p. 143)

Kenner finds Emma "like Dante's Beatrice [in that] she manifests in [Stephen's] earthly experience the Church Triumphant of his spiritual dream" (p. 130).

deliverance from the egoism which, without their being fully aware of it, encapsulates them. To cope with the former aspect of their predicament Frédéric and Stephen must find creative vocations, and to remedy the latter they must discover how to love. The life instinct propels them toward the elusive power of regeneration they require in forms of the eternal feminine, *das Ewig-Weibliche*. These forms include both the Beatrices, such spiritual ideals as Mme Arnoux and Mercedes, and the Cleopatras, such sensual women as *la Maréchale* and the Nighttown prostitute. Neither of the young men succeeds in reconciling the conflicting needs to which these divergent types respond. Joyce expresses the paradoxical position not only of his own character, Stephen, but also, to a lesser extent, of Frédéric as well in letters to his wife Nora:

"One moment I see you like a virgin or madonna the next moment I see you shameless, insolent, half naked and obscene! . . .

"Guide me, my saint, my angel. Lead me forward. *Everything* that is noble and exalted and deep and true and moving in what I write comes, I believe, from you. O take me in your soul of souls and then will I become indeed the poet of my race. . . . My body will soon penetrate into yours, O that my soul could too! O that I could nestle in your womb like a child born of your flesh and blood, be fed by your blood, sleep in the warm secret gloom of your body!"[42]

The last lines point toward Bloom, crouching in foetal position alongside Molly in the *Ithaca* episode of *Ulysses*, toward the acceptance of woman as of the

---

[42] *Letters of James Joyce*, ed. Stuart Gilbert and Richard Ellmann (New York, 1957-1966), II, 243, 248. The letters are dated September 2 and 5, 1909, i.e., while work on the *Portrait* was in progress.

earth, earthy. This is the direction, Joyce indicates, that Stephen must travel if he is to secure the moral poise indispensable to his art. At the last instant in which we see Frédéric, however, he insists more emphatically than ever on the necessity of holding the ideal and the actual apart, lest Dulcinea turn into mere Aldonza Lorenzo. Of Flaubert himself, Philip Spencer recounts that "the last night of the old year he always spent in a brothel as a gesture of cynicism, but he derived no pleasure from it; he picked out the ugliest girl and made love to her with a cigar still in his mouth, just to show his friends how little he cared. In fact it showed how much, in other circumstances, he might have cared."[43] Since the attempt to realize one's dreams has as its ineluctable result disillusionment, Flaubert's hero must protect his ideal by refusing Mme Arnoux's invitation in the penultimate chapter. Only so long as the youthful enchantments of the heart remain uncorrupted by experience may one be called fortunate: "c'est là que nous avons eu de meilleur" (612).[44]

[43] *Flaubert* (New York, 1953), p. 51.
[44] "That was the happiest time we ever had" (419).

CHAPTER IV

SEA CHANGES

THE RENDERING OF
INWARD EXPERIENCE
IN *MADAME BOVARY*
AND *PROTEUS*

Full fathom five thy father lies;
  Of his bones are coral made;
Those are pearls that were his eyes:
  Nothing of him that doth fade
But doth suffer a sea-change
Into something rich and strange.

—The Tempest

Paris, plus vaste que l'Océan,
miroitait donc aux yeux d'Emma
dans une atmosphère vermeille.[1]

—Madame Bovary

A seachange this, brown eyes
saltblue. Seadeath, mildest of
all deaths known to man. Old
Father Ocean.

—Ulysses

the *Wake* may be more ambitious in their conception, but, if achieved form constitutes the decisive proof of value, they must be relegated to a second order of eminence. It seems justifiable, then, to devote both this chapter and the one following to a comparison of the two *opera maxima*.

Few critics would deny that the most significant development in the novel during the past century has been the discovery of new techniques for a sustained and intensive probing of mental life. In this connection, we may note that the appearance of *Ulysses* in 1922 had an impact on the literary world comparable to the profound tremor which accompanied the publication of *Madame Bovary* sixty-five years before. Both novels revealed approaches to the presentation of psychological aspects of character which substantially reshaped the craft of fiction in their times.

Rather than rehearse the general observations on the two writers' techniques which have been made so often, I shall compare in this chapter several aspects of the representational modes in part I, Chapter IX of *Madame Bovary* and *Proteus*, the third episode of *Ulysses*, with an eye toward pinpointing some areas in which Flaubert anticipates Joyce as well as remarking important respects in which they diverge. The two chapters are strategically situated within their respective novels. If we regard the structures of *Madame Bovary* and *Ulysses* as instances of musical form, we find that each chapter falls at the end of the first of three movements in a symphonic progression. Chapter IX is the last in part I, and is thus the point at which Flaubert draws together all the major themes emerging from the narrative of Charles' and Emma's childhoods, marriage, visit to La Vaubyessard, and life in Tostes; it also prepares for the second movement, which begins with the Bovarys' arrival in Yonville. *Proteus* concludes Joyce's

Telemachia, the segment of *Ulysses* devoted to Stephen Dedalus. We witness a similar resolution—temporary and exceedingly precarious, to be sure—of the themes generated in the course of Stephen's encounters in *Telemachus* and *Nestor* and a prefiguration of Bloom's advent. (One may note that both Flaubert and Joyce create a suspense of anticipation by delaying the entrance of their principal characters until the novels are well underway.) The crucial rapprochement between the two chapters, for our purposes, is the fact that very little action takes place in them; they are given over to an exploration of the subjective life of Emma and Stephen at a point when each character is undergoing a pronounced transformation of feeling.

Flaubert's stylistic mastery serves the needs of psychological portraiture to excellent effect. Consider the image with which Chapter ix opens: "Souvent, lorsque Charles était sorti, elle allait prendre dans l'armoire, entre les plis du linge où elle l'avait laissé, le porte-cigares en soie verte."[4] The syntactical suspense—the object withheld till the end, the complicated clausal modification, the emphasis created by setting the sentence off in its own paragraph—would have made Henry James envious. Flaubert sketches the action in a few swift strokes which suggest a great deal. Emma's growing sense of detachment from her husband and the deception she comes to practice on him are implicit in the green silk cigar case she hides among piles of linen. The cigars, which choke Charles when he tries to smoke them, are obviously emblematic of the manly attributes she finds lacking in him. The case itself, the only

---

[4] *Madame Bovary* (Paris: Conard, 1910), p. 79. Subsequent page references will appear in parentheses in the text.
"Often when Charles was out she went to the closet and took the green silk cigar case from among the piles of linen where she kept it" (63).

tangible remnant of her taste of aristocratic living at La Vaubyessard, becomes for her a symbol of *le grand monde*.

In the following sentence Flaubert recounts that Emma would look at the case, open it, and even sniff its odor of verbena and tobacco. These simple acts and sensations stimulate her fancy in much the same way romantic fiction does. At this moment the point of view shifts from the impersonal observer to the interior of Emma's mind: "A qui appartenait-il? . . . Au vicomte" (79). Flaubert effects the transition without a break in the continuity of style. Not only does Emma imagine that the case belonged to the vicomte with whom she waltzed at La Vaubyessard, but she speculates that it was the gift of his mistress. She goes on to embroider fancifully the circumstances of its manufacture, her reverie reaching a maudlin peak: "Un souffle d'amour avait passé parmi les mailles du canevas; chaque coup d'aiguille avait fixé là une espérance ou un souvenir, et tous ces fils de soie entrelacés n'étaient que la continuité de la même passion silencieuse" (79).[5] Lest any doubt remain as to the real identity of the vicomte's imaginary mistress, Flaubert has Emma's musings move without pause from the presentation of the cigar case to the reflection that "elle était à Tostes. Lui, il était à Paris, maintenant; là-bas" (79)! Paris—"quel nom démesuré!" (80)[6]—has evocative powers even stronger than the *porte-cigares* and sends her along a new train of thought that runs for three pages.

Let us now turn to a passage in *Proteus* in which

[5] "Love had breathed through the mesh of the canvas; every stroke of the needle had recorded a hope or a memory; and all these intertwined silken threads bespoke one constant, silent passion" (64).

[6] "She was in Tostes. Whereas he, now, was in Paris—in Paris! . . . The very name had such a vastness about it" (64)!

Joyce practices a similar stylistic sleight of hand and which should furnish us with a basis for making some important distinctions between the novelists' handling of subjective points of view in these chapters. In this episode Stephen walks along Sandymount strand contemplating the perpetual flux he perceives in nature, in language, and above all in himself. He has responded to the call of art, but his vocation has yet to bear fruit and he is tormented by self-doubt. Feelings of guilt about his mother's death also plague him. These considerations among others prompt him to question his courage, moral and physical. There are frequent indications in the sections of *Ulysses* in which Bloom and Molly are dominant that water represents the life force, and in the first chapter Buck Mulligan, who loves the sea and is an excellent swimmer, has characterized the flood as "our mighty mother."[7] Stephen, who holds his Falstaffian companion in contempt, is forced to admit, comparing himself with Mulligan, that "he saved men from drowning and you shake at a cur's yelping" (45).

The following fifteen lines, in which we are wholly within the flow of Stephen's consciousness, deserve scrutiny. Discomfited by his unflattering perception about himself, Stephen engages in an internal dialogue. At first he tries to repress the insight by disparaging Mulligan, who has ridiculed him as a posturer: "But the courtiers who mocked Guido in Or san Michele were in their own house. House of . . ." Stephen's conscience, which is a harsh one, interrupts: "We don't want any of your medieval abstrusiosities. Would you do what he did?" His ego, protean in its agility, attempts another evasion: "A boat would be near, a lifebuoy." The superego declares sarcastically, *"Natürlich,*

7 *Ulysses* (New York: Modern Library, 1961), p. 5. Subsequent page references will be incorporated in the text.

put there for you. Would you or would you not?" Stephen's deep fear of the force that he feels is threatening
him surfaces in his recollection of a fatal incident:
"The man that was drowned nine days ago off Maiden's
rock, they are waiting for him now." But his impulse
to self-examination will not relent: "The truth, spit it
out." Finally his full mind yields in a torrent of anguished candor:

"I would want to. I would try. I am not a strong
swimmer. Water cold soft. When I put my face into
it in the basin at Clongowes. Can't see! Who's behind
me? Out quickly, quickly! Do you see the tide flowing
quickly in on all sides, sheeting the lows of sand
quickly, shellcocoacoloured? If I had land under my
feet. I want his life still to be his, mine to be mine. A
drowning man. His human eyes scream to me out of
horror of his death. I . . . With him together down . . .
I could not save her. Waters: bitter death: lost." (45-
46)

The stylistic ruse of Flaubert—"Elle était à Tostes.
Lui, il était à Paris"—finds a parallel in Joyce's "With
him together down . . . I could not save *her*." The
anonymous "him" is metamorphosed into what is evidently a maternal "her" and the tense shifts from present to past. Stephen's feeling of guilt regarding his
mother's death, not so much a belief that his prayers
would have improved the lot of her soul as a sense of
the sheer cruelty of failing to humor her at a time when
she was, as Mulligan says, picking "buttercups off the
quilt" (8), emerges from his unconscious to torture
him. It seems plain too that Stephen identifies with the
drowning victim as surely as does Emma with the
vicomte's mistress, albeit in his case unwillingly.

The different uses Flaubert and Joyce make of the
device of substituted identity are revealing. The former

employs it to confirm what the reader has already sus-
pected about Emma and to effect a transition to the
Parisian revery without the dislocation of point of view
an overt authorial intrusion would entail. In *Proteus*
the shift from "him" to "her" injects a new theme into
the reflections on the rescue of a drowning man, one
which is integrated in this particular context only
through the associative process of Stephen's mind. The
theme of obsessive guilt crops up unexpectedly at a
number of places in the novel, each time expanding
our awareness of its importance for Stephen.[8] Flaubert's technique, in this instance, exercises the reader's
capacity for immediate perception rather than his
memory. His substitution is much more restricted in
its significance, although no less pleasing as a means
of engendering surprise.

The technical points I have been discussing in connection with these passages have far-reaching implications. Perhaps the most important of these is the
question of authorial distance, or, conversely, the im-
mediacy of the material being presented. I remarked
earlier that the point of view in the second paragraph
of Chapter IX is situated within Emma's mind. That,
however, is only half the truth. What we are given is,
to be sure, the content of her consciousness, but *not*
exactly in the way it occurs to her. Flaubert's style intervenes. Emma herself lacks the sensitivity and intelligence required to phrase her thoughts and feelings in
the precise, beautifully cadenced prose we find here.
Erich Auerbach declares, in the course of his explica-
tion of another passage in the same chapter, that "there

---

[8] Consider, for example, Stephen's anguished and ineffectual
response to the plight of his sister Dilly, the mother in little,
in *Wandering Rocks*: "She is drowning. Agenbite. Save her.
. . . She will drown me with her, eyes and hair" (243).

is nothing of Flaubert's life in these words, but only Emma's; Flaubert does nothing but bestow the power of mature expression upon the material which she affords, in its complete subjectivity. If Emma could do this herself, she would no longer be what she is, she would have outgrown herself and thereby saved herself."[9] This statement strikes me as being apposite to virtually all the instances of subjective point of view in *Madame Bovary*. Flaubert offers us, then, a double perspective. Remaining as artist impartial, impersonal, and objective, he allows us to see things through Emma's view and, at the same time, frames her subjective vision with a language of extraordinary richness. The contrast serves to point up and evaluate her fatuity and pathos. At the same time, the form provides us with an achieved artistic harmony which is its own reward.

Joyce grants us much fuller access to Stephen's consciousness via the interior monologue. The term "interior monologue" satisfies hardly anyone, but no one has produced a better one to describe the type of narration which confronts us in *Proteus*. Robert Humphrey offers a definition which has the virtues of being simple and reasonably accurate: "Interior monologue is, then, the technique used in fiction for representing the psychic content and processes of character, partly or entirely unuttered, just as these processes exist at various levels of conscious control before they are formulated for deliberate speech."[10] The language in the passage

---

[9] *Mimesis*, trans. Willard Trask (Princeton Univ. Press, 1953), p. 484. Auerbach's whole discussion (pp. 482-90) of what he terms "the objective seriousness" of Flaubert's representational mode is illuminating. See also Jean Rousset, *Forme et signification* (Paris, 1962), pp. 185-208.

[10] *Stream of Consciousness in the Modern Novel* (Berkeley and Los Angeles, 1959), p. 24.

we have been considering does in fact imitate the manner of Stephen's thought. He is a literary intellectual,
accustomed to thinking dialectically in conventional
syntactical units. Given his divided mind, it is natural
then that he should cast his reflections in the form of
a dialogue. As his rational defenses give way before the
onslaught of fear and guilt, though, he abandons or-
derly phraseology and falls into a staccato rhythm of
free association. We have here an example of what
Joyce called "the dramatic form,"[11] in which the author
does not come between his characters and the reader.

When the character through whose point of view the
narration is taking place succumbs to confusion, acute
problems of understanding and judgment present
themselves to the reader. The interior monologue does
not afford Joyce the kind of ordering matrix that Flaubert's objective style provides. Of the controls Joyce
brings to bear on his depiction of Stephen's psychic
state, the use of motifs, recurring images and symbols,
seems especially important. These devices also find extensive application in *Madame Bovary*. A comparison
of the ways in which they are employed in the two
novels should prove illuminating.

More than any other novelist of the nineteenth century, Flaubert is responsible for the de-emphasis of
plot and action characteristic of so much of the best
modern fiction. His stated ambition to produce "a book
dependent on nothing external, which would be held
together by the strength of its style,"[12] led him to devise

[11] *A Portrait of the Artist as a Young Man*, ed. Chester Anderson and Richard Ellmann (New York, 1964), p. 215.

[12] *The Selected Letters of Gustave Flaubert*, trans. and ed.
Francis Steegmuller (New York, 1953), p. 127 (*Correspondance* [Paris: Conard, 1926-1933], ii, 345). The statement appears in a letter to Louise Colet dated January 16, 1852, i.e.,
during an early phase of the composition of *Madame Bovary*.

a very intricate network of interrelated symbols and images in order to develop and unify his novel. *Madame Bovary* stands beside *Les Fleurs du mal* as one of the pioneer works of art embodying a *forêt de symboles*. No writer has pursued the tradition initiated by Baudelaire and Flaubert further than Joyce in the "daedal networks" of *Ulysses* and *Finnegans Wake*.

Let us now consider one representative strand of thematic imagery occurring in Chapter IX. Emma listens to the fishmongers who pass through Tostes at night and reflects that the next day they will arrive in Paris, the imaginative center of her universe. "Et elle les suivait dans sa pensée, montant et descendant les côtes, traversant les villages, filant sur la grande route à la clarté des étoiles. Au bout d'une distance indéterminée, il se trouvait toujours une place confuse où expirait son rêve" (80).[13] The picture Flaubert creates gives a universality to Emma's mood of longing and, at the same time, underscores her isolation. The last sentence establishes firmly the distance between Emma and her author, "l'ermite de Croisset"; a principal source of her frustration is the fact that her dreams issue forth from an undisciplined and second-rate imagination. In an earlier chapter Flaubert has informed us that her temperament is "plus sentimentale qu'artiste, cherchant des émotions et non des paysages" (50), and, in one of the rare instances of overt authorial judgment in Chapter IX, he remarks that "elle confondait, dans son désir, les sensualités du luxe avec les joies du coeur, l'élégance des habitudes et les délicates-

---

[13] "And she followed them in thought, up and down hills, through villages, along the highway by the light of the stars. Then, somewhere along the way, her dream always petered out" (64).

ses du sentiment" (82).[14] He need not have resorted to direct commentary to record Emma's undiscriminating taste; her mediocrity is evaluated in the image of a "place confuse où expirait son rêve." (One should not confound her longings with the aspirations of the symbolists toward an elusive ideal of beauty. Emma craves the excitement of Paris, not Mallarmé's *azur*.) The image of a disappearing view recurs frequently in this chapter, in which her growing sense of the oppressiveness of her surroundings and her desire to escape them are major themes. The following are prominent occurrences:

> Paris, plus vaste que l'Océan, miroitait donc aux yeux d'Emma dans une atmosphère vermeille. (81)

> [Parisian society] était une existence au-dessus des autres, entre ciel et terre, dans les orages, quelque chose de sublime. Quant au reste du monde, il était perdu, sans place précise, et comme n'existant pas. (82)

> Tout ce qui l'entourait immédiatement, campagne ennuyeuse, petits bourgeois imbéciles, médiocrité de l'existence, lui semblait une exception dans le monde, un hasard particulier où elle se trouvait prise, tandis qu'au delà s'étendait à perte de vue l'immense pays des félicités et des passions. (82)

> Comme les matelots en détresse, elle promenait sur la solitude de sa vie des yeux désespérés, cher-

[14] "Her temperament was more sentimental than artistic, and what she was looking for was emotions, not scenery" (41).

"In her longing she made no difference between the pleasures of luxury and the joys of the heart, between elegant living and sensitive feeling" (66).

chant au loin quelque voile blanche dans les
brumes de l'horizon. (87)

L'avenir était un corridor tout noir, et qui avait
au fond sa porte bien fermée. (87)

Au loin, parfois, un chien hurlait: et la cloche, à
temps égaux, continuait sa sonnerie monotone qui
se perdait dans la campagne. (88)[15]

The first passage suggests lines early in *Le Père
Goriot*: "Mais Paris est un véritable océan. Jetez-y la
sonde, vous n'en connaîtrez jamais la profondeur."[16]
Emma, one recalls, derives her impressions of Paris
largely from the novels of Balzac and George Sand.
Significantly, Balzac urges the reader to plumb the
depths to the extent that his capacities permit; Emma
is able to see only the surface and that in a rosy light.

[15] "Paris, city vaster than the ocean, glittered bfore Emma's
eyes in a rosy light" (65).
"Everything immediately surrounding her—boring countryside, inane petty bourgeois, the mediocrity of daily life—seemed
to her the exception rather than the rule. She had been caught
in it all by some accident: out beyond, there stretched as far
as eye could see the immense territory of rapture and passions"
(66).
"Like a sailor in distress, she kept casting desperate glances
over the solitary waste of her life, seeking some white sail in
the distant mists of the horizon" (69).
"The future was a pitch-black tunnel, ending in a locked
door" (70).
"Far off somewhere a dog was howling. And the bell would
keep on giving its regular, monotonous peals that died away
over the countryside" (71).
[16] Honoré de Balzac, *Oeuvres complètes* (Paris, 1956), IV,
45: "But Paris is a veritable ocean. Though you heave the
sounding lead into it, you will never know its depth" (my translation). Margaret B. Tillett, *On Reading Flaubert* (London,
1961), pp. 26-27, suggests this connection and the following
one with Baudelaire, although she does not develop the point.
It is she who calls attention to most of the images of distance
quoted above.

The fourth quotation anticipates the "matelots oubliés dans une île" of *Le Cygne*.[17] In her own way Emma is as much in exile from the France of Louis-Philippe as are Hugo, Baudelaire, and Flaubert from that of Louis Napoleon. (These echoes are worth noting since they prefigure the allusive technique Joyce practices on a massive scale. His deliberate and systematic integration of allusions into his structure of motifs invites the reader to bring to bear on *Ulysses* the standards of judgment embodied in the allusive material and thus provides one of the organizing principles. Even in *Madame Bovary*, though, the effect is an added richness of reference.)

The primary function of these images of disappearing view, as I hope was evident in my discussion of the first of them in the *mareyeurs* passage, is to offer us the sort of controlled and penetrating insight into Emma's psyche that no amount of straight description could furnish. The ironic counterpointing of the luxuriant prose in which they are cast and the poverty of Emma's condition serves perfectly to evaluate her longings in a manner at once wry and poignant. Frequent varied repetition within a relatively short space does much to define the theme and tone of the chapter.

Nowhere in *Ulysses* do image- and symbol-motifs play a more crucial role in establishing structural coherence than in the third episode. Joyce's dominant theme in this section, one must recall, is the protean transformations of the phenomenal world. It is not simply flux, though, which concerns him, but also the patterns or principles underlying mutability, the "ineluc-

[17] Charles Baudelaire, *Oeuvres complètes* (Paris, 1961), p. 83: "sailors forgotten on an island." The date of *Le Cygne* is 1859, so there is no question of Flaubert's having borrowed from Baudelaire, although the reverse is at least possible.

table modalities" of the audible and visible. Recurring images constitute one form of these modalities and are among the "signatures of all things I am here to read" (37).

Above all Stephen is in search of his self: "I threw this ended shadow from me, manshape, ineluctable, call it back. Endless, would it be mine, form of my form?" (48) His quest is accompanied by a profound distrust of life and, as we have seen, dread of death. In the course of the chapter, Stephen eventually does arrive at a point of emotional stasis, however momentary. The entire episode takes place in the hour from eleven to noon. Toward the end of it, Stephen, warmed by the "southing sun" at its apex, grows calm. In a phrase suggesting Mallarmé's *L'Après-midi d'un faune*,[18] he muses that it is "Pan's hour, the faunal noon. Among gumheavy serpentplants, milkoozing fruits, where on the tawny waters leaves lie wide. Pain is far" (49). To emphasize this shift of mood Joyce has him repeat to himself a line from Yeats's "Who Goes with Fergus?": *"And no more turn aside and brood"* (49). By italicizing the quotation and setting it off in a separate paragraph, Joyce obviously intends to give the sentiment considerable weight.

Shortly beyond this point the image of the drowning victim which we considered earlier appears once more: "A corpse rising saltwhite from the undertow, bobbing landward, a pace a pace a porpoise. . . ."

"Bag of corpsegas sopping in foul brine. A quiver of minnows, fat of a spongy tidbit, flash through the slits of his buttoned trouserfly. God becomes man becomes fish becomes barnacle goose becomes featherbed moun-

[18] W. Y. Tindall, *A Reader's Guide to James Joyce* (New York, 1959), p. 149, points out this relationship.

tain. Dead breaths I living breathe, tread dead dust, devour a urinous offal from all dead. Hauled stark over the gunwale he breathes upward the stench of his green grave, his leprous nosehold snoring to the sun.

"A seachange this, brown eyes saltblue. Seadeath, mildest of all deaths known to man. Old Father Ocean." (50)

Stephen has come a long way in a short time. One can hardly read this passage as a vision of delight, but one need only compare the frightened ellipses of the "waters: bitter death" meditation with the sonorous rhythms of these reflections to apprehend the change that has taken place. Stephen can now contemplate the prospect of death, ugly as it is, with an attitude approaching resignation.

Stephen's thoughts parody Hamlet's graveyard speech. Joyce has even gone Shakespeare one better. Hamlet's king, who does a progress through the guts of a beggar, has become the God-man incarnate in Featherbed Mountain in the Wicklow Hills. Stephen may lack the prince's Christian stoic trust in the providence that attends the fall of a sparrow, but he shares fully his fondness for grim jests. In the next paragraph Stephen, who in the *Portrait* echoed the prince of hell's defiant *non serviam*, reflects, "Allbright he falls, proud lightning of the intellect, *Lucifer, dico, qui nescit occasum*. No. My cockle hat and staff and his my sandal shoon. Where? To evening lands. Evening will find itself" (50). The pilgrim's "cockle hat" and "sandal shoon" (*Hamlet*, IV.v.25) make the identification explicit. To metamorphose oneself from Lucifer into Hamlet is scarcely to make peace with the world, but at any rate it places one's destiny on a nobler foundation. The Hamlet analogue is at least as pervasive in *Ulysses* as

the Telemachus parallel[19] and perhaps even more apposite.

Another Shakespeare allusion in the passage under
consideration is somewhat more problematic. The "sea-
change" plainly refers to the teasing ditty Ariel sings
to Ferdinand in *The Tempest* (1.ii.396ff). On the preceding page Stephen has quoted a full line from the
song—"Full fathom five thy father lies"—perhaps asso-
ciating his own father, very much a drifter, with the
drowning man.[20] Stephen's "bag of corpsegas" has, however, few affinities, except of the most ironic sort, with
the green world of *The Tempest*. A great gap exists
between the youthful intensity of *Hamlet* and the
mature serenity of Shakespeare's late romance, and
Stephen is not prepared to bridge it, at least not yet.

If anyone in *Ulysses* may be compared with Prospero,
it is Bloom. "Seadeath, mildest of all deaths known to
man" is just the sort of observation Leopold might
make (albeit "scientifically" rather than poetically).
Bloom accepts death matter-of-factly: "Once you are
dead you are dead" (105). He sees it as an inevitable
phase of the life-cycle and a source of renewal. Standing in Glasnevin cemetery at the same hour Stephen
paces Sandymount stand, he observes, "The Botanic

---

[19] William M. Schutte, *Joyce and Shakespeare* (New Haven,
1957), p. 191, catalogues 88 quotations or adaptations of quotations from Hamlet in *Ulysses*. By far the largest number of
references (42) is attributed to Stephen.

One feels that Flaubert would have endorsed warmly Joyce's
selection of models for his protagonists, for he remarked that
"Ulysses is perhaps the greatest type in all ancient literature,
and Hamlet in all modern" (*Selected Letters*, p. 156; *Correspondance*, III, 257).

[20] Note also a comparable allusion to "Lycidas" in the same
paragraph: "Sunk though he be beneath the watery floor" (50).
In the Nestor episode Stephen has heard a schoolboy recite
three lines of the elegy (p. 26).

Gardens are just over there. It's the blood sinking in the earth gives new life. Same idea those jews they said killed the christian boy" (108). His eventual end does not in the least deter him from affirming life: "Plenty to see and hear and feel yet. . . . They are not going to get me this innings. Warm beds: warm fullblooded life" (115). Stephen's phrase "devour a urinous offal from all dead" implies disgust. Shortly thereafter, we learn that "most of all [Bloom] liked grilled kidneys which gave to his palate a fine tang of faintly scented urine" (55). Joyce might well have gone to school with Flaubert to acquire this technique of ironic counterpoint.[21] In any case, the allusion to *The Tempest* appears to look forward to Bloom's arrival on the next page of the novel. Indeed Stephen's whole shift of attitude in the last two pages of *Proteus* seems calculated to prepare for his advent. Stephen, the spiritual orphan, needs desperately to move toward the mature self-possession Bloom represents. And the Wandering Jew is in search of a son.

Joyce demonstrates brilliantly, in his treatment of this and other crucial motifs in *Ulysses*, the validity of employing image patterns in lieu of dramatic action to depict character development. His strategy of bringing to bear on Stephen's mind a variety of converging perspectives renders a richly complex definition of character. We encounter Bloom in the same way, and discover that in his case Joyce has raised the technique to the tenth power, yielding a personage often cited as

[21] Cf. one instance of Flaubert's similar use of ironic contrast with Emma and Charles: "Elle se sentait, d'ailleurs, plus irritée de lui. Il prenait, avec l'âge, des allures épaisses . . . il faisait, en avalant sa soupe, un gloussement à chaque gorgée" (86). Emma's ennui and frustrated dreams are juxtaposed with Charles's enjoyment of their married life, the opposition being a very important structural support in the chapter.

the most fully realized in all fiction. A survey of the
continuing critical controversy over just what attitude
Joyce intends us to take toward his protagonists will
quickly convince one of the hazards inherent in Joyce's
method and, even more, of the strain it imposes on his
readers. The passage I have just discussed seems to
me one of the keys to a more affirmative interpretation
of Stephen than has generally been offered. The ironic
humor with which he manages to confront the spectre
of death on this occasion indicates that he is beginning
to come to terms with his private demon. If we read
the passage in this light, the parallel with Hamlet does
not diminish Stephen, but rather confers on him a
measure of the prince's dignity.

It would not do to discuss the ninth chapter of
Madame Bovary without considering the celebrated
image of the burning bouquet with which Flaubert
concludes the first part of the novel. The disappearing-
view motif dealt with earlier is a fine example of Flaubert's use of a recurring image to assist in establishing
a specific theme within a given chapter (significant instances of it do, of course, occur outside of Chapter ix,
particularly in the scene in which Rodolphe seduces
Emma). The destruction of Emma's wedding bouquet
has a much broader function: it is a complex symbolic
action which draws together and expresses in concen-
trated form several dominant concerns in part i and
adumbrates developments in the remainder of the book.

The last paragraph save one opens with the matter-
of-fact observation that "un jour qu'en prévision de son
départ elle faisait des rangements dans un tiroir, elle
se piqua les doigts à quelque chose" (94).[22] This is the
first view of Emma we have following Charles' decision

[22] "One day when she was going through a drawer in prepa-
ration for moving, something pricked her finger" (76).

to leave Tostes, the village she so detests that it has caused her to sink into an emotional and finally a physical malaise. A scant page before, we have witnessed Emma cursing God and weeping over what she considers the injustice of her fate. The sentence quoted above appears, then, curiously lacking in intensity, given a turn of affairs that seems to promise relief. Then we discover that the mere "quelque chose" which pricks her finger is in fact the wire of her bridal bouquet. Its yellowed orange blossoms are emblematic of her tarnished hopes and its tattered ribbons of her frayed emotions.

In addition to the conventional symbolism of a wedding bouquet, Emma's has acquired a peculiar significance. Upon first entering Bovary's house at Tostes, she has seen "sur le secrétaire, près de la fenêtre . . . dans une carafe, un bouquet de fleurs d'oranger, noué par des rubans de satin blanc. C'était un bouquet de mariée, le bouquet de l'autre! Elle le regarda" (44). Charles had forgotten to dispose of the first Madame Bovary's nosegay. His oversight is a paradigm of the gaucheries which weigh so heavily on Emma. Flaubert recounts that "Emma songeait à son bouquet de mariage, qui était emballé dans un carton, et se demandait, en rêvant, ce qu'on en ferait, si par hasard elle venait à mourir" (44-45).[23] This incident Léon Bopp calls *présymbolique*[24]—a useful term to indicate the process whereby Flaubert invests images which are to recur at

[23] "On the desk near the window, standing in a decanter and tied with a white satin ribbon, was a bouquet of orange blossoms—a bride's bouquet: the *other* bride's bouquet! She stared at it . . . and thought of her own bridal bouquet, which was packed in one of those very boxes, wondering what would be done with it if she were to die" (36-37).

[24] *Commentaire sur "Madame Bovary"* (Neuchâtel, 1951), p. 119.

crucial points in the narrative with a symbolic value.

When Emma pricks her finger on the wire, hidden like a serpent's fangs among the blossoms, and then throws the bouquet into the fire, we recognize that the gesture signifies the moral and psychological death of her marriage. Flaubert records the act laconically and then gives us an extraordinary, detailed description of the bouquet in flames:

"Il s'enflamma plus vite qu'une paille sèche. Puis ce fut comme un buisson rouge sur les cendres, et qui se rongeait lentement. Elle le regarda brûler. Les petites baies de carton éclataient, les fils d'archal se tordaient, le galon se fondait; et les corolles de papier, racornies, se balançant le long de la plaque comme des papillons noirs, enfin s'envolèrent par la cheminée." (94)[25]

"Elle le regarda brûler" recalls the entranced gaze with which she viewed Nastasie's bouquet. It is, as Margaret Tillett points out, "the fixed abstract gaze of the habitual daydreamer."[26]

The image suggests Emma's desire to eradicate the memory of a bleak period in her life. Even more important, it embodies a portent of the destruction her extravagance is to wreak. The "buisson rouge" prophesies the conflagration which will consume not just Emma herself but Charles and Berthe as well. (Flaubert informs us, in the curt sentence which ends the chapter, that madame is pregnant when she leaves Tostes. For Emma, the child is a bitter reminder.) Ironically, one of the subordinate images in the picture foreshadows

[25] "It blazed up quicker than dry straw. Then it lay like a red bush on the ashes, slowly consuming itself. She watched it burn. The pasteboard berries burst open, the brass wire curled, the braid melted; and the shriveled paper petals hovered along the fireback like black butterflies and finally flew away up the chimney" (76).

[26] On Reading Flaubert, p. 28.

a moment of enjoyment—her cab ride with Léon in Rouen. The "papillons noirs" look forward to the fragments of a letter Emma throws from a window, "qui se dispersèrent au vent et s'abattirent plus loin, comme des papillons blancs . . ." (338).[27] The blackness of the butterflies in the earlier image presages, however, the illusory quality of her happiness in the latter instance. The total effect of the image of the burning bouquet points overwhelmingly to the ultimate catastrophe of this woman who wishes to live like Cleopatra and ends by dying like Antony.

The symbolist tactic Flaubert employs here, the use of an image at a major turning point in the novel to crystallize theme, finds a Joycean counterpart in the last paragraph of *Proteus*. Having arrived at the state of relative poise I discussed in connection with the "bag of corpsegas" passage, Stephen prepares to return to the city. Before departing, however, "he turned his face over a shoulder, rere regardant. Moving through the air high spars of a threemaster, her sails brailed up on the crosstrees, homing, upstream, silently moving, a silent ship" (51). "Rere regardant" describes Stephen's vision aptly. His introspection always involves a good deal of historical retrospection. For once, though, he is looking at an object outside himself. The ship, we learn in *Wandering Rocks*, is "the threemasted schooner *Rosevean*" (249), and among its crew is W. B. Murphy, who is returning home to his wife after seven years at sea (608). The discovery that this Odysseus figure was aboard provides confirmation, if any is needed, that

[27] "The wind caught them and scattered them, and they alighted at a distance, like white butterflies . . ." (279). John C. Lapp, "Art and Hallucination in Flaubert," *French Studies*, x (1956), reprinted in Raymond Giraud, ed., *Flaubert* (Englewood Cliffs, N.J., 1964), pp. 83-84, calls attention to this correspondence.

CHAPTER V

JEUNES FILLES EN FLEURS

SPATIAL FORM IN *MADAME BOVARY* AND *NAUSICAA*

De temps à autre, il partait une pauvre chandelle
romaine; alors la foule béante poussait une
clameur où se mêlait le cri des femmes à qui
l'on chatouillait la taille pendant l'obscurité.
Emma, silencieuse, se blottisait doucement
contre l'épaule de Charles; puis, le menton levé,
elle suivait dans le ciel noir le jet lumineux
des fusées. Rodolphe la contemplait à la
lueur des lampions qui brûlaient.[1]

—Madame Bovary

And she saw a long Roman candle going up over
the trees up, up, and, in the tense hush, they were
all breathless with excitement as it went higher
and higher and she had to lean back more
and more to look up after it, high, high,
almost out of sight, and her face was suffused
with a divine, an entrancing blush from straining
back and he could see her other things too,
nainsook nickers, the fabric that
caresses the skin.   *—Ulysses*

I'll be a candle-holder, and look on.

—Romeo and Juliet

CHAPTER V

JEUNES FILLES EN FLEURS

SPATIAL FORM IN *MADAME BOVARY*

AND *NAUSICAA*

$\mathcal{A}$s the preceding chapter suggests, one of the great services Flaubert performed for fiction was to liberate it from what E. M. Forster has characterized as "tyranny by the plot."[2] That is not to say, of course, that *Madame Bovary* is a plotless or an action-less novel. Flaubert maintains a continuous narrative line through most of the book and at a half dozen key points employs full-blown dramatic scenes to advance the story. The attenuation of plot is much more marked in *Ulysses*, although even there the dramatic development

---

[1] "Now and then some pathetic little Roman candle would go off and bring a roar from the gaping crowd—a roar amidst which could be heard the screams of women, fair game for ticklers in the darkness. Emma nestled silently against Charles's shoulder, raising her head to follow the bright trail of the rockets in the black sky. Rodolphe watched her in the glow of the colored lamps." (*Madame Bovary*, trans. Francis Steegmuller [New York, 1957], p. 173. All translated passages are from this edition.)

[2] *Aspects of the Novel* (Harmondsworth, Middlesex, 1962), p. 109.

of character continues to play an essential role.[3] Indeed it is difficult to imagine how a novel of almost eight hundred pages could attain unity without relying to some extent on story values. The fact remains, however, that after Flaubert narrative no longer constituted the core of fiction.

Madame Bovary and *Ulysses* both depend upon multiple structures, upon an orchestration of effects that gives the two works a rigor and a density which are not to be found in the traditional novel. Perhaps for that reason commentators have felt obliged to draw analogies with poetry and painting and music in their analyses of the two books. As we have seen, the use made of motifs in *Madame Bovary* laid the foundation for the labyrinthine networks of *Ulysses*. The technique has much more obvious affinities with symbolist verse and Wagnerian opera than it does with the practice of earlier European novelists. In a seminal essay, Joseph Frank describes the displacement of consecutive narration entailed in the large scale use of cross-references as "spatialization" of fiction. Such writers as Proust and Joyce, Frank holds, intend the reader "to apprehend their work spatially, in a moment of time, rather than as a sequence."[4] One must attempt to perceive the significant patterns in a novel simultaneously, to hold together in one's mind all the components of what Pound terms the "Image"—"that which presents an intellectual and emotional complex in an instant of time."[5] It is the characteristic mode of the plastic arts.

---

[3] S. L. Goldberg's *The Classical Temper* (London, 1961), to my mind the soundest study of *Ulysses* yet to appear, lays heavy stress on the dramatic aspect of the novel.

[4] "Spatial Form in Modern Literature," in *The Widening Gyre* (Bloomington, Ind., 1968), p. 9.

[5] *Literary Essays of Ezra Pound*, ed. T. S. Eliot (London, 1954), p. 4. A. Walton Litz discusses very lucidly the doctrine

The spatial method presents a formidable challenge to the memory, ingenuity, and patience of the reader, who must arrange the fragmentary associations that run through the minds of Joyce's characters in a pattern that approximates the author's controlling design. His reward consists in a heightened sense of satisfaction when the pieces finally fall into place and the book discloses its "Image." The narrative of the characters' immediate experiences on Bloomsday, presented in chronological order, sustains the reader while he is exploring the spatial form and is its complement in the overall structure of the work.[6]

The questions we have been considering with regard to *Ulysses* are in large measure applicable to *Madame Bovary*. Frank begins his discussion of aesthetic form in the modern novel by invoking the celebrated *Comices agricoles* (part II, Chapter VIII) as an early instance of the tendency that concerns him. All the major and many of the minor characters participate in this scene, either actively or in the thoughts of others. The action and dialogue occur simultaneously on three strata: *le peuple* and their livestock in the square, the officials on the platform, and Emma and Rodolphe observing

---

of the "Image" as one key to the form of *Ulysses* and *Finnegans Wake* in *The Art of James Joyce* (London, 1961), pp. 53-62.

[6] It would surely be mistaken to insist that the reader must comprehend every detail of *Ulysses* before the controlling design reveals itself. Robert M. Adams declares sanely that "the reader who confronts this novel like a rational novel reader and not like a compulsive idiot must necessarily sense only in passing the little details of verbal by-play, the little patterns of fact and fiction, the buried allusions and errors. As a novel reader, he is in pursuit of more significant game; as the reader of a novel constructed on epic lines, he has all sorts of parallels, counterparts, balanced ironies, and lines of development to keep his appreciative faculties occupied" (*Surface and Symbol* [New York, 1962], p. 246).

the whole spectacle from the second floor of the town hall. Flaubert cuts cinematically from one plane to another in a manner that dissolves sequence. "For the duration of the scene, at least," comments Frank, the time-flow of the narrative is halted: a tension is fixed on the interplay of relationships within the limited time-area. These relationships are juxtaposed independently of the progress of the narrative; and the full signifi-cance of the scene is given only by the reflexive rela-tions among the units of meaning. . . . The unit of meaning is not, as in modern poetry, a word-group or a fragment of an anecdote, but the totality of each level of action taken as an integer. . . . But this does not affect the parallel between aesthetic form in mod-ern poetry and the form of Flaubert's scene. Both can be properly understood only when their units of mean-ing are apprehended reflexively in an instant of time."[7] Flaubert himself was well aware of the novelty of the undertaking. "It's a difficult section," he remarked in a letter to Louise Colet. "But if I succeed, it will be truly symphonic."[8]

Finding instances of "symphonic" or spatial tech-nique in *Ulysses* which parallel closely the *Comices* scene poses no great problem. The tenth chapter, *Wan-dering Rocks*, is, like the *Comices*, situated in the mid-dle of the book and serves in an analogous manner as a microcosm of Joyce's fictional world; nineteen time-related views are given us of Dubliners watching a prog-ress of the British viceroy through the city streets. *Circe*,

---

[7] *The Widening Gyre*, pp. 15-16. Frank appears to regard the *Comices* as an isolated example of spatial technique in *Madame Bovary*, but John C. Lapp points out a number of similar, if less dazzling, instances ("Art and Hallucination in Flaubert," *French Studies*, x [1956], reprinted in *Flaubert*, ed. Raymond Giraud [Englewood Cliffs, N.J., 1964], pp. 79ff).

[8] *Correspondance* (Paris: Conard, 1926-1933), iii, 335 (my translation).

the fifteenth chapter, in which the themes, events, and personages that impinge on the psychic lives of Bloom and Stephen find expression in a bizarre hallucinatory drama, also offers grounds for comparison. But since there is a still closer rapprochement between the methods of *Circe* and *La Tentation de saint Antoine*, I prefer to reserve consideration of the episode for the next chapter.

Perhaps the segment of *Ulysses* which may be juxtaposed most fruitfully with the *Comices* is the thirteenth chapter, *Nausicaa*. The situations Flaubert and Joyce depict in these scenes correspond: in each case we witness an illicit flirtation set against a ceremonial backdrop—speech-making and prize-giving in the *Comices* and a Mass and pyrotechnics in *Nausicaa*. In addition Joyce presents us with a character, Gerty MacDowell, who so strikingly resembles Flaubert's heroine that we may think of her as Emma's Irish grand-niece. The similarities and, more important, the differences between the male protagonists in these chapters do much to illumine the satiric intentions of the two novelists. As in the *Comices*, the principal elements of *Nausicaa* —in particular the interior monologues of Gerty and Bloom—are integers which counterpoint each other ironically. "Joyce may be musical in taste rather than pictorial," reflects Frank Budgen, "yet his view of life is that of a painter surveying a still scene rather than that of a musician following a development through time." And for no portion of *Ulysses* does this observation hold truer than for *Nausicaa*. The "art" of this episode in Joyce's elaborate table of correspondences is painting, and indeed "everything, moving and stationary, affirms the idea of space."[9]

Flaubert's technique of juxtaposition is very effec-

[9] *James Joyce and the Making of "Ulysses"* (Bloomington, Ind., 1960), pp. 153, 213.

tively realized in the two-page passage which begins when prefectural councilor Lieuvain arrives at the peroration of a flatulent address praising agriculture and the Orleanist regime. The councilor, who is an archetypal hack politician, has just called his listeners' attention to recent improvements in flax production. Flaubert interrupts to remark that "il n'avait pas besoin de l'appeler: car toute les bouches de la multitude se tenaient ouvertes, comme pour boire ses paroles."[10] At this point we are treated to a view of the various observant attitudes struck by the notables of Yonville-l'Abbaye: Tuvache's wide-eyed gaze, Derozerays' gently flickering lids, Homais' hand cupped to his ear so as not to lose a syllable of the discourse, and the other jury members' chins nodding slowly against their vests "en signe d'approbation." Then the camera pans the ranks below:

"Les pompiers, au bas de l'estrade, se reposaient sur leurs baïonettes; et Binet, immobile, restait le coude en dehors, avec la pointe du sabre en l'air. Il entendait peut-être, mais il ne devait rien apercevoir à cause de la visière de son casque qui lui descendait sur le nez. Son lieutenant, le fils cadet du sieur Tuvache, avait encore exagéré le sien; car il en portait un énorme et qui lui vacillait sur la tête, en laissant dépasser un bout de son foulard d'indienne. Il souriait là-dessous avec une douceur tout enfantine, et sa petite figure pâle, où des gouttes ruisselaient, avait une expression de jouissance, d'accablement et de sommeil." (202)[11]

---

[10] *Madame Bovary: moeurs de province* (Paris: Conard, 1910), p. 202. Subsequent page references will appear in parentheses in the text. "There was no need for him to 'call their attention': every mouth in the crowd was open, as though to drink in his words" (164).

[11] "The fire brigade, at the foot of the platform, leaned on their bayonets; and Binet stood motionless, elbow bent, the tip

Flaubert's mockery is relatively restrained and at times playful when he deals with robust and simple folk. His portrait of Tuvache's son is if anything affectionate. But these rustics remain on the periphery; it is the bourgeois who almost constantly occupy the foreground. And for them the latter-day Saint Polycarp reserves his most mordant satire.

Flaubert concludes the paragraph devoted to the peasants by describing cows "arrachant avec leur langue quelque bribe de feuillage qui leur pendait sur le museau" (203). The image looks forward to the passage in the next chapter in which Rodolphe pulls away the ferns caught in Emma's stirrup and the moment when "le drap de sa robe s'accrochait au velours de l'habit . . . et, défaillante, tout en pleurs, avec un long frémissement et se cachant la figure, elle s'abandonna" (223).[12] In the *Comices* scene, Flaubert turns

---

of his sword in the air. He could hear, perhaps, but he certainly could not see, for the visor of his helmet had fallen forward onto his nose. His lieutenant, who was Monsieur Tuvache's younger son, had gone him one better: the helmet he was wearing was far too big for him and kept teetering on his head and showing a corner of the calico nightcap he had on under it. He was smiling from beneath his headgear as sweetly as a baby; and his small pale face, dripping with sweat, wore an expression of enjoyment, exhaustion and drowsiness" (164).

[12] "A cow would bellow as her tongue tore off some bit of foliage hanging down over her muzzle" (165).

"The broadcloth of her habit clung to the velvet of his coat . . . and, her resistance gone, weeping, hiding her face, with a long shudder she gave herself to him" (181).

Rodolphe's removal of the ferns (220) recalls vividly the times during Emma's wedding day when thistles caught in her gown: "elle enlevait les herbes rudes avec les petits dards des chardons, pendant que Charles, les mains vide, attendait qu'elle eût fini" (37)/ "at such moments she would carefully pick off the coarse grasses and thistle spikes with her gloved fingers, as Charles waited empty-handed beside her" (31). In contrast

directly from the masticating cow to Rodolphe, who is laying the groundwork for his conquest: "Les instincts les plus nobles, les sympathies les plus pures sont persécutés, calomniés, et, s'il se rencontre enfin deux pauvres âmes, tout est organisé pour qu'elles ne puissent se joindre" (203).[13] In his insistence on the validity of embattled passion and his subsequent assertion that fate will assure its success, Rodolphe shrewdly exploits Emma's romanticism. Having been privy to his decision to seduce her, the reader knows, as she does not, that his affirmations are utterly insincere and that he is no more than a cold sensualist.

The rapid shifts of focus from the officials to the common people to Rodolphe convey, insofar as the consecutive nature of language permits, a sense of our witnessing a multiplicity of simultaneous occurrences. When we move on to Emma, however, a new dimension is added, for Flaubert affords us an inside view of her reactions as Rodolphe speaks. In her mind, past and (without her being aware of it) future converge on the present. A languor comes over her, and the sensations of the moment lead her to recall some of the emotional highlights of her generally drab life. Rodolphe's pomade reminds her of the vicomte with whom she waltzed at La Vaubyessard, just as did the cigar case discussed in the preceding chapter. At this instant she perceives the Hirondelle slowly descending a distant hill, "en traînant après soi un long panache de poussière" (204). The old stagecoach is to play a

---

to Charles, Rodolphe leans gracefully from his saddle to assist her as they ride along.

[13] "The noblest instincts, the purest sympathies are persecuted and dragged in the mud; and if two poor souls do find one another, everything is organized to keep them apart" (165).

significant part in her many rendezvous with Léon in Rouen; even now she associates it with the clerk:

"C'était dans cette voiture jaune que Léon, si souvent, était revenu vers elle; et par cette route là-bas qu'il était parti pour toujours! Elle crut le voir en face, à sa fenêtre; puis tout se confondit, des nuages passèrent; il lui sembla qu'elle tournait encore dans la valse, sous le feu des lustres, au bras du vicomte, et que Léon n'était pas loin, qu'il allait venir . . . et cependant elle sentait toujours la tête de Rodolphe à côté d'elle. La douceur de cette sensation pénétrait ainsi ses désirs d'autrefois, et comme des grains de sable sous un coup de vent, ils tourbillonnaient dans la bouffée subtile du parfum qui se répandait sur son âme." (204)[14]

The commingling of past and present, the disposition to transpose objects of desire, and the images of whirling and dissolution are, as we have seen, hallmarks of Flaubert's romantic protagonists. Emma's revery breaks off and the clock begins moving again as she hears M. Lieuvain concluding his speech: "Continuez! persévérez!" the councilor urges, "n'écoutez ni les suggestions de la routine, ni les conseils trops hâtifs d'un empirisme

[14] "The Hirondelle [descended], trailing a long plume of dust behind it. It was in this yellow carriage that Léon had so often returned to her; and that was the road he had taken when he had left forever. For a moment she thought she saw him across the square, at his window; then everything became confused, and clouds passed before her eyes; it seemed to her that she was still whirling in the waltz, under the blaze of the chandeliers, in the vicomte's arms, and that Léon was not far off, that he was coming. . . . And yet all the while she was smelling the perfume of Rodolphe's hair beside her. The sweetness of this sensation permeated her earlier desires, and like grains of sand in the wind these whirled about in the subtle fragrance that was filling her soul" (166).

téméraire!" (204)[15] He is talking about soil improve-
ment and animal husbandry; indirectly, though, his
words offer Emma both encouragement to break out of
a domesticity she finds stultifying and warning against
impetuous, superficial judgments. For the moment she
is able to maintain a tenuous balance, but it is one that
Rodolphe will experience little difficulty in overturn-
ing.

We have already seen the extent to which Frédéric
Moreau's values and expectations are shaped by the
romantic fiction he has read. Mme Bovary possesses
the same trait in at least equal measure. Quickly dis-
enchanted with her marriage to Charles, "Emma cher-
chait à savoir ce que l'on entendait au juste dans la
vie par les mots de *félicité*, de *passion* et d'*ivresse*, qui
lui avaient paru si beaux dans les livres" (47).[16] She
believes that their meaning "dans la vie" has disclosed
itself when she becomes Rodolphe's lover and, charac-
teristically, she identifies her new role with its fictive
models:

"Alors elle se rappela les héroïnes des livres qu'elle
avait lus, et la légion lyrique de ces femmes adultères
se mit à chanter dans sa mémoire avec des voix de
soeurs qui la charmaient. Elle devenait elle-même
comme une partie véritable de ces imaginations et réal-
isait la longue rêverie de sa jeunesse, en se considé-
rant dans ce type d'amoureuse qu'elle avait tant envié."
(225-226)[17]

---

[15] " 'Persist!' he was saying. 'Persevere! Follow neither the
beaten tracks of routine nor rash counsels of reckless empiri-
cism' " (166).

[16] "Emma tried to imagine just what was meant, in life, by
the words 'bliss,' 'passion,' and 'rapture'—words that had seemed
so beautiful to her in books" (39).

[17] "She remembered the heroines of novels she had read, and
the lyrical legion of those adulterous women began to sing in

We are, Hugh Kenner observes, at "the center of the maze, where life and art are uncertain which copies the other. . . . *Madame Bovary* is a novel about a woman who reads novels, kept as close as possible to the plot, the characterization, and the dialogue of the sort of novels she has read."[18] Flaubert's book thus takes its place in the great tradition of parodic fiction stemming from Cervantes.

The crucial distinction between *Madame Bovary* and the popular romances lies, as I suggested in the last chapter, in Flaubert's stylistic transformation of his material. Joyce's parody in *Nausicaa* and several other episodes of *Ulysses* reduces the distance between the satiric target and the form which imitates it. We witness a shift from Flaubert's *style indirect libre* to the mode of indirect interior monologue.[19] There remain, of course, the exaggerated effects which prevent us from confusing the satire with its object, but Joyce's rendering of a shop-girl's consciousness makes Flaubertian grace inappropriate. Gerty MacDowell's monologue is cast, Joyce told Budgen, in "a namby-pamby jammy marmalady drawsery (alto la!) style with effects of incense, mariolatry, masturbation, stewed cockles, painter's palette, chitchat, circumlocutions, etc., etc."[20] The

---

her memory with sisterly voices that enchanted her. Now she saw herself as one of those *amoureuses* whom she had so envied: she was becoming, in reality, one of that gallery of fictional figures; the long dream of her youth was coming true" (183).

[18] *Flaubert, Joyce and Beckett: The Stoic Comedians* (Boston, 1962), pp. 23, 22.

[19] For a discussion of how the concept of an "indirect" interior monologue applies to *Nausicaa*, see Robert Humphrey, *Stream of Consciousness in the Modern Novel* (Berkeley and Los Angeles, 1962), pp. 29-31.

[20] *Letters of James Joyce*, ed. Stuart Gilbert and Richard Ellmann (New York, 1957-1966), I, 134.

reader must depend chiefly on Bloom's half of the episode and on the critical context established by the work as a whole to place Gerty in the proper perspective (although, as we shall see, there are several normative poles of Joyce's irony embedded directly in her monologue).

A pennyworth of her thoughts should suffice to show her affinity with Emma:

"Had kind fate but willed her to be born a gentlewoman of high degree in her own right and had she only received the benefit of a good education Gerty MacDowell might easily have held her own beside any lady in the land and have seen herself exquisitely gowned with jewels on her brow and patrician suitors at her feet vying with one another to pay their devoirs to her. Mayhap it was this, the love that might have been, that lent to her softlyfeatured face at whiles a look, tense with suppressed meaning, that imparted a strange yearning tendency to the beautiful eyes a charm few could resist. Why have women such eyes of witchery? Gerty's were of the bluest Irish blue, set off by lustrous lashes and dark expressive brows. Time was when those brows were not so silkilyseductive. It was Madame Vera Verity, directress of the Woman Beautiful page of the Princess novelette, who had first advised her to try eyebrowleine which gave that haunting expression to the eyes, so becoming in leaders of fashion, and she had never regretted it."[21]

One has the sense, reading a passage such as this, that he is seeing Emma's soul *mise à nue*, unredeemed by Flaubert's imagery and cadences. Gerty's *Bovarysme*, the self-intoxication induced by overreading, derives

---

[21] *Ulysses* (New York: Modern Library, 1961), pp. 348-349. Subsequent page references will appear in parentheses in the text.

not only from the romances she borrows from the lending library but also from the advertising slogans that
seem to have infiltrated every corner of her mind. Thus
she is confident that "those iron jelloids she had been
taking of late had done her a world of good much better than the Widow Welch's female pills and she was
much better of those discharges she used to get and
that tired feeling" (348). In this respect she appears
to be a spiritual descendant of the pharmacist Homais,
who offers a toast "à l'industrie et aux beaux arts, ces
deux soeurs!" (213).[22]

In Joyce's scheme of analogues for the characters
and events of his novel, Gerty's sentimental eroticism
finds its counterpart and counterpoint in the good sense
of Nausicaa, the chaste princess of Naxos who attends
to the needs of the naked, barnacle-encrusted Odysseus.
In the *Odyssey* we come upon Nausicaa at the seaside,
where she supervises her maids as they wash linen.
Correspondingly, Joyce informs us that "as for undies
they were Gerty's chief care" (350). He also establishes
an ironic parallel between his "girlwoman" and the Virgin Mary, "her who is in her pure radiance a beacon
ever to the storm-tossed heart of man" (346). As a matter of fact, Gerty's petticoats, which beckon Bloom, are
blue—the Virgin's color[23]—and bits of the litany of Our
Lady of Loreto, which is being sung at a nearby chapel,
are interspersed with her thoughts. While the priests
exhibit the Sacrament, she puts on a show of her own
for Bloom, who sits on the beach watching:

"Then they sang the second verse of the *Tantum ergo*
and Canon O'Hanlon got up again and censed the
Blessed Sacrament and knelt down and he told Father

---

[22] "To those twin sisters, industry and the fine arts!" (174).
[23] W. Y. Tindall, *A Reader's Guide to James Joyce* (New
York, 1959), p. 196, points out this correspondence.

Conroy that one of the candles was just going to set fire to the flowers and Father Conroy got up and settled it all right and she could see the gentleman winding his watch and listening to the works and she swung her leg more in and out in time. . . . She knew by the feel of her scalp and the irritation against her stays that that thing must be coming on because the last time too was when she clipped her hair on account of the moon. His dark eyes fixed themselves on her again and drinking in her every contour, literally worshipping at her shrine." (361)

The similarity between the satirical juxtaposition Joyce employs here and that of Flaubert in the passage depicting the three layers of society should be evident. There is an even closer rapprochement between the facet of *Nausicaa* represented by the quotation above and the segment of the *Comices* in which Flaubert syncopates M. Derozerays' awarding of prizes with Rodolphe's blandishments to Emma—one of the *loci classici* of the novel. "Cent fois même j'ai voulu partir, et je vous ai suivie, je suis resté," Rodolphe affirms. "Fumiers," says the chairman, as if to tell Emma that she should be holding her nose rather than her companion's hand. The counterpoint continues in the same vein:

—Comme je resterais ce soir, demain, les autres jours, toute ma vie!
"A M. Caron, d'Argueil, une médaille d'or!"
—Car jamais je n'ai trouvé dans la société de personne un charme aussi complet.
"A M. Bain, de Givry-Saint-Martin!"
—Aussi, moi, j'emporterai votre souvenir.
"Pour un belier mérinos . . ."
—Mais vous m'oublierez, j'aurai passé comme une ombre.

"A M. Belot, de Notre-Dame . . ."

—Oh! non, n'est-ce pas, je serai quelque chose dans votre pensée, dans votre vie?

"Race porcine, prix *ex aequo* à MM. Lehérissé et Cullembourg; soixante francs!" (206-207)[24]

And so on, with Derozerays' unwitting barbs punctuating each of Rodolphe's fervent protestations.

Flaubert delivers a symbolic *coup de grâce* to the entire assemblage with the presentation of a silver medal to Catherine Leroux. The medal, worth twenty-five francs, is all the recognition her fifty-four years of service on the same farm have earned her. Her gnarled hands offer "l'humble témoignage de tant de souffrances subies. Quelque chose d'une rigidité monacale relevait l'expression de sa figure. Rien de trieste ou d'attendri n'amollissait ce regard pâle. Dans la fréquentation des animaux, elle avait pris leur mutisme et leur placidité. . . . Ainsi se tenait, devant ces bourgeois épanouis," declares Flaubert apocalyptically, "ce demi-siècle de servitude" (208-209).[25] Catherine shares

---

[24] "A hundred times I was on the point of leaving, and yet I followed you and stayed with you . . ."

"For the best manures."

". . . as I'd stay with you tonight, tomorrow, every day, all my life!"

"To Monsieur Caron, of Argueil, a gold medal!"

"Never have I been so utterly charmed by anyone . . ."

"To Monsieur Bain, of Givry-Saint-Martin!"

". . . so that I'll carry the memory of you with me . . ."

"For a merino ram . . ."

"Whereas you'll forget me: I'll vanish like a shadow."

"To Monsieur Belot, of Notre-Dame . . ."

"No, though! Tell me it isn't so! Tell me I'll have a place in your thoughts, in your life!"

"Hogs: a tie! To Messieurs Lehérissé and Cullembourg, sixty francs!" (168).

[25] "They hung half open, as though offering their own humble testimony to the hardships they had endured. A kind of

with Dr. Larivière, the surgeon who comes to examine Emma on her deathbed, the possession of unimpeachable integrity. Her very being stands as a reproach to the shoddiness and hypocrisy of life in Yonville. The faithful old servant's true reward consists in the "sourire de béatitude" that crosses her face when she decides to sacrifice her prize.

Catherine Leroux's presence in the *Comices* provides a much more unequivocal standard against which the other characters may be judged than does the Mass in *Nausicaa*. The Mass culminates a men's temperance retreat, an event which, as the *"Tantum ergo"* passage suggests and Joyce's story "Grace" more clearly indicates, cannot be regarded as particularly edifying. Apparently the Virgin herself constitutes the ideal with which we are to contrast Gerty, but that too may be questioned. Joyce's later work, from *Exiles* on, points toward his acceptance of a much earthier ideal of *das Ewig-Weibliche*. He conceived of Molly Bloom as a "sane full amoral fertilisable untrustworthy engaging shrewd limited prudent indifferent *Weib. Ich bin das Fleisch das stets bejaht!*"[26] In her undiscriminating, sensual affirmation of life, Molly complements masculine intellectuality and skepticism. The latter traits are represented in their most extreme form by Stephen Dedalus, who frequently plays the Mephistophelian *Geist, der stets verneint.* If Molly is the feminine norm, then Gerty's principal failing lies perhaps in her confining her eroticism too largely to fantasy. It is Bloom,

---

monklike rigidity gave a certain dignity to her face, but her pale stare was softened by no hint of sadness or human kindness. Living among animals, she had taken on their muteness and placidity. . . . Thus did half a century of servitude stand before these beaming bourgeois" (169-170).

[26] *Letters*, I, 170.

however, who scrutinizes Gerty most intensively, and it is to him that Joyce entrusts the main thrust of his criticism—and appreciation—of her.

Commentators sometimes complain that Flaubert and Joyce have treated their *jeunes filles* with excessive severity. Flaubert, says Matthew Arnold, "is cruel, with the cruelty of petrified feeling, to his poor heroine; he pursues her without pity or pause, as with malignity; he is harder upon her himself than any reader even, I think, will be inclined to be."[27] And S. L. Goldberg concludes that "Joyce's ironic parody is breaking a butterfly on its wheel."[28] The two novelists might possibly have overdone their satire, but they are by no means so unrelenting as these statements imply.

Flaubert carefully dissociates himself from Rodolphe's callousness toward Emma. In one of his infrequent editorial intrusions, he censures her lover's lack of understanding:

"Il ne distinguait pas, cet homme si plein de pratique, la dissemblance des sentiments sous la parité des expressions. . . . Comme si la plénitude de l'âme ne débordait pas quelquefois par les métaphores les plus vides, puisque personne, jamais, ne peut donner l'exacte mesure de ses besoins, ni de ses conceptions, ni de ses douleurs, et que la parole humaine est comme un chaudron fêlé où nous battons des mélodies à faire danser les ours, quand on voudrait attendrir les étoiles." (265)[29]

27 *Works of Matthew Arnold* (London, 1903), IV, 203.
28 *The Classical Temper*, p. 141.
29 "He had no perception—this man of such vast experience —of the dissimilarity of feeling that might underlie similarities of expression. . . . Whereas the truth is that fullness of soul can sometimes overflow in utter vapidity of language, for none of us can ever express the exact measure of his needs or his thoughts or his sorrows; and human speech is like a cracked

Flaubert sympathizes with the essential romantic aspiration to transcend the conditions of quotidian existence, although he disapproves of many of the forms the impulse assumes and effects it produces. Emma's yearning for a life superior to that afforded by Yonville elevates her above nearly all the other characters in the novel and, given the measure of dignity conferred by Flaubert's style, even renders her capable of tragedy.[30]

Although Gerty is at times undeniably pathetic, Joyce never permits us to regard her as anything but comic. The comedy is not, however, invariably hostile. If Joyce intended merely to satirize such an easy mark, we would have to agree that he had trained his sixteen-inch guns on a skiff. The *beau idéal* Gerty longs for is distinctly paternal. She wants "a manly man with a strong quiet face who had not found his ideal, perhaps his hair sligthly flecked with gray, and who would understand" (351), and she thinks she may have found him in Bloom. Though vitiated by sentimentality, Gerty's vision of Bloom is perhaps the most consistently sympathetic in the whole of *Ulysses*. (Even Molly ad-

---

kettle on which we tap crude rhythms for bears to dance to, while we long to make music that will melt the stars" (216).

[30] Emma is, of course, guilty of the same failure of sympathy, which is essentially a failure of imagination, as Rodolphe. Thus she remains unaware of the depth of feeling underlying Charles's regularized transports: "incapable, du reste, de comprendre ce qu'elle n'éprouvait pas, comme de croire à tout ce qui ne se manifestait point par des formes convenues, elle se persuada sans peine que la passion de Charles n'avait plus rien d'exorbitant" (61)/ "since she was incapable of understanding what she didn't experience, or of recognizing anything that wasn't expressed in conventional terms, she reached the conclusion that Charles's desire for her was nothing very extraordinary" (49).

mits, though, that one of the reasons she married him was that "he understood or felt what a woman is," 782.)

Bloom's interior monologue does not present him as exactly the "dreamhusband" Gerty has in mind, but it does reveal that he is sensitive to the needs of her sex as well as responsive to its attractions. Her lameness elicits his compassion: "Poor girl! That's why she's left on the shelf and the others did a sprint. Thought something was wrong by the cut of her jib. Jilted beauty. A defect is ten times worse in a woman" (367-368). But on this occasion Leopold is no sentimentalist: "Sad about her lame of course but must be on your guard not to feel too much pity," he muses. "They take advantage" (377). In any case, her handicap does not seriously detract from her charms: "Glad I didn't know about it when she was on show," he admits, then reflects, "Hot little devil all the same. Wouldn't mind. Curiosity like a nun or a negress or a girl with glasses" (368). And the attention she lavishes on her lingerie is not wasted, for Bloom knows how to enjoy "a dream of wellfilled hose" (368).[31]

The pyrotechnic display which concludes the agricultural fair in *Madame Bovary* fizzles, since the rockets have gotten damp. The fireworks at the Mirus bazaar in *Nausicaa* are wetter still but hardly a failure. Toward the close of Gerty's segment of the chapter a missile reaches its apogee: "And then a rocket sprang and bang shot blind and O! then the Roman candle burst and it was like a sigh of O! and everyone cried O! O! in raptures and it gushed out of it a stream of

---

[31] Rodolphe appreciates Emma's hosiery too; he contemplates "la délicatesse de son bas blanc, qui lui semblait quelque chose de sa nudité" (221)/ "her sheer white stocking that showed . . . as though it were a bit of her naked flesh" (179).

rain gold hair threads and they were all green dewy
stars falling with golden, O so lively! O so soft, sweet,
soft!" (366-367). A moment before this event "her
woman's instinct told her that she had raised the devil
in him" (360). A little while later Bloom confirms her
intuition: "O Lord, that little limping devil. Begins to
feel cold and clammy. Aftereffect not pleasant. Still you
have to get rid of it someway. . . . My fireworks. Up
like a rocket, down like a stick" (370-371). The style,
at once matter of fact and wry, in which his thoughts
find expression, neatly undercuts the breathless, nov-
elettish prose apposite to Gerty. At the same time, Joyce
engages in self-parody, as any reader who recalls the
wading girl epiphany in *A Portrait* can easily recognize.[32]

Bloom may not be the chevalier, the "man of inflexi-
ble honour to his fingertips" (365), that Gerty sup-
poses, but he is at least "thankful for small mercies"
(368). He regards his encounter with her and the resultant orgasm as a consolation for the rebuffs dealt
him during the day. Nonetheless his onanism represents an offense against fertility. (In the debate at the
lying-in hospital he opposes the use of contraceptives.)
Because of feelings of incapacity related to the death
of his infant son Rudy, Joyce's hero has not had inter-
course with his wife for eleven years, and this unnat-
ural abstinence has generated acute difficulties. One
that recurs in his thoughts all day is the liaison between
Molly and her concert manager, Blazes Boylan. Many
times in the course of *Nausicaa* we see Bloom inspect
his watch, which has stopped at half past four—the
hour of Molly and Boylan's assignation. He tries in a

[32] Richard Ellmann, *James Joyce* (New York, 1959), p. 370,
comments perceptively on the relationship between these
scenes.

number of ways to reconcile himself to this unpleasant
fact, even going so far as to speculate that it might
really be nothing more than a commercial transaction:
"Suppose he gave her money. Why not? All a prejudice.
She's worth ten, fifteen, more a pound. All that for nothing" (369). Bloom's role in *Nausicaa* recalls a passage
in Stephen's interpretation of *Hamlet*: "The playwright
who wrote the folio of this world . . . would be bawd
and cuckold too but that in the economy of heaven,
foretold by Hamlet, there are no more marriages, glori-
fied man, an androgynous angel, being a wife unto
himself" (213).

Bloom's cuckoldry has obvious affinities with Charles
Bovary's. Both bear part of the responsibility for their
wives' adultery in that they have failed to satisfy the
women's sexual needs. Bloom is the more to blame, since
he knows what those needs are. His imaginary pimp-
ing for her follows, perhaps, from his recognition of
that fact and finds a parallel in Charles' unwitting act
of procurement on Emma's behalf. Charles insists that,
for the sake of her health, she accept "les propositions
de M. Boulanger, qui sont si gracieuses." When her new
riding habit arrives, he writes Rodolphe that "sa femme
était à sa disposition, et qu'il comptait sur sa complai-
sance" (218).[33] Flaubert's handling of the dramatic
irony at this point is exceedingly adept. Charles remains ignorant of his wife's duplicity until after her
death, but when he does discover it he attributes it to
circumstances beyond human control and absolves
Emma and her lover. All the same, the knowledge
erodes the vestiges of his will to survive.

[33] " 'Why don't you accept Monsieur Boulanger's suggestions?
He's being so gracious.' . . . Charles wrote to Monsieur Boulanger that his wife was at his disposition, and that they thanked
him in advance for his kindness" (177).

Bloom's devotion to Molly does not reach the hound-like docility of Charles's, but it is nonetheless genuine. And he is far more realistic and resilient in his accept-ance of what is, after all, a *fait accompli*. When Leo-pold repossesses his home at the end of the day, equa-nimity and abnegation conquer envy and jealousy in his mind:

"Equanimity?

"As natural as any and every natural act of a nature expressed or understood executed in natured nature by natural creatures in accordance with his, her and their natured natures, of dissimilar similarity. As not as calamitous as a cataclysmic annihilation of the planet in consequence of collision with a dark sun. As less rep-rehensible than theft, highway robbery, cruelty to chil-dren and animals. . . . As more than inevitable, irrep-arable." (733)

His tolerance and understanding of Molly's actions are expressive of "mute immutable mature animality" (734). In that pithy phrase Joyce indicates the essen-tial base upon which his notion of adult love is founded. The necessity of moral freedom in relations between men and women, specifically husbands and wives, which is the theme of *Exiles*, undergoes a comic meta-morphosis in *Ulysses*: "Greater love than this," says Stephen in a drunken paraphrase of John 15:13, "no man hath that a man lay down his wife for his friend" (393). By this criterion, Bloom is entitled to share Catherine Leroux's *sourire de béatitude*.

One cannot forget, though, that *Nausicaa* is one epi-sode in which Bloom's role as a sacrificial victim re-mains in the background. For once the initiative can be his, if he chooses to take it. Leopold considers the desirability of a future rendezvous with Gerty and ac-tually begins to leave a message for her in the sand.

"I. AM. A." (381) he writes, then effaces the letters. His failure to follow the "A" with a substantive has prompted some ingenious speculations on the part of commentators. W. Y. Tindall thinks it possible that "Bloom's 'A' stands for Alpha (or God)."[34] Deifying Bloom seems, to say the least, far-fetched, but there *is* an advantage in reading the "A" as alpha. Earlier in the day, while walking on the same stretch of beach, Stephen has placed an umbilical telephone call across history: "The cords of all link back, strandentwining cable of all flesh. . . . Hello. Kinch here. Put me on to Edenville. Aleph, alpha: nought, nought, one" (38). Stephen spends June 16, 1904, looking for a spiritual father. And Bloom is never more paternal than when he eschews the temptation to meet Gerty again. In the next episode, *Oxen of the Sun*, Telemachus/Stephen and Ulysses/Bloom finally come together at the maternity hospital, although, as in Homer, there is no immediate recognition on the part of the former that his long-distance call has gotten through.

In contrast with the good sense and essential decency Bloom displays in not following up his encounter with Gerty, Rodolphe's decision to seduce Emma prefigures all the sordidness and cruelty of their affair. His analysis of Emma's vulnerability is acute enough, as far as it goes:

"Et on s'ennuie! on voudrait habiter la ville, danser la polka tous les soirs! Pauvre petite femme! Ça bâille après l'amour, comme une carpe après l'eau sur une table de cuisine. Avec trois mots de galanterie, cela vous adorerait, j'en suis sûr! ce serait tendre! charmant! . . . Oui, mais comment s'en débarrasser ensuite?" (181)[35]

---

[34] *A Reader's Guide to James Joyce*, p. 195.
[35] "How bored she must be! Dying to live in town, to dance

These reflections would not be out of place in Bloom's mind, but the difference lies in Rodolphe's failure to weigh the implications of the liaison from Emma's standpoint. As Gerty hopes and Molly knows, Leopold is a man who understands and cares about others, a man, like Lear, "more sinned against than sinning" (358).

Flaubert concludes the *Comices* chapter with Homais' article in the *Fanal de Rouen*. The pharmacist recapitulates the happenings at the fair in a style whose verve puts the ordinary Bastille Day orator or chamber-of-commerce pamphleteer to shame: "Pourquoi ces festons, ces fleurs, ces guirlandes? Où courait cette foule, comme les flots d'une mer en furie, sous les torrents d'un soleil tropical qui répandait sa chaleur sur nos guérets?" (212-213)[36] Having generated a keen sense of anticipation with these questions, he goes on to lecture the government on its duty to rural areas and then describes the councilor's arrival, not forgetting to mention the martial splendor of the brigade. When he lists the jury members, he adds a footnote to his own name reminding readers of his monograph on cider and depicts "en traits dithyrambiques" the joy of the prize-winners. The fireworks, he says, led one to imagine that Yonville had been transported "au milieu d'un rêve des *Milles et une nuits*" (214). Lest anyone suppose that this *Arabian Nights* atmosphere lent

---

the polka every night! Poor little thing! She's gasping for love like a carp on a kitchen table gasping for water. A compliment or two and she'd adore me, I'm positive. She'd be sweet! But— how would I get rid of her later?" (147)

[36] "Why these festoons, these flowers, these garlands? Whither was it bound, this crowd rushing like the billows of a raging sea under a torrential tropic sun that poured its torrid rays upon our fertile meadows?" (173)

itself to improprieties, Homais assures his readers that "aucun événement fâcheux n'est venu troubler cette réunion de famille" (214).[37]

Homais' article serves as more than a humorous capstone to a brilliant comic scene. We are invited, especially by the reference to "cette réunion de famille," to juxtapose his perspective on the *Comices* with the events Flaubert has depicted—particularly Rodolphe and Emma's dalliance—and to see it as still another strand in the vast web of illusion which ensnares the principals in *Madame Bovary*. And this juxtaposition of divergent viewpoints lies at the core of spatial form.

The ending of *Nausicaa* also depends upon the reader's simultaneous perception of the elements in an intellectual and emotional complex. Joyce assists him by bringing the crucial components into focus with the cooing of a cuckoo clock. Bloom's hour on the strand leaves him exhausted, and at the close of it he dozes off. As he does so, some of the thoughts that have passed through his mind during the day recur in fragmentary form. Most of them, for example, "met him pike hoses" and "frillies for Raoul," are in some way associated with female sexuality, especially Molly's. While Bloom naps, a bat flies past him. In *A Portrait*, we may recall, the bat represents Irish womanhood "waking to the consciousness of itself in darkness and secrecy and loneliness,"[38] and it suggests also the awakening of an artist to his calling. The bat's significance seems analogous in *Ulysses*, except that darkness, secrecy, and loneliness are attributes of Bloom's condition

[37] "Our modest village imagined itself transported into the midst of an Arabian Nights dream. . . . No untoward incidents arose to disturb this family gathering" (174).

[38] *A Portrait of the Artist as a Young Man*, ed. Chester Anderson and Richard Ellmann (New York: Viking, 1964), p. 221.

too. But then, as one of his fellow Dubliners remarks, "There's a touch of the artist about old Bloom" (235).

His monologue reaches its terminus, and the two other integers of the episode make their final appearance. The clergy have finished celebrating the Mass and are now consuming another "frugal meal":

>*Cuckoo*
>*Cuckoo*
>*Cuckoo*

The clock on the mantelpiece in the priest's house cooed where Canon O'Hanlon and Father Conroy and the reverend John Hughes S. J. were taking tea and sodabread and butter and fried mutton chops with catsup and talking about

>*Cuckoo*
>*Cuckoo*
>*Cuckoo*

Because it was a little canary bird that came out of its little house to tell the time that Gerty Mac-Dowell noticed the time she was there because she was as quick as anything about a thing like that, was Gerty MacDowell, and she noticed at once that that foreign gentleman that was sitting on the rocks looking was

>*Cuckoo*
>*Cuckoo*
>*Cuckoo*   (382)

The clock is the same one that Gerty remembers having seen in the rectory on another occasion. Bloom's portion of the episode begins when she rises to leave the strand. The fact that she is still within sight of him indicates that the fifteen pages devoted to his thoughts represent only a few minutes of chronometric time. In any case, Gerty's blithely chirping "canary" is a bird of another feather to Bloom. The "cuckoo"—"O word of fear!" (212)[39]—announces his cuckoldry: natural, inevitable, irreparable.

[39] Cf. *Love's Labour's Lost*, v, ii, 908: "Cuckoo, cuckoo; O, word of fear,/ Unpleasing to a married ear!"

CHAPTER VI

THE NETHERMOST ABYSS

EXPRESSIONISM IN
*LA TENTATION DE SAINT
ANTOINE* AND *CIRCE*

Thither he plies
Undaunted to meet there whatever power
Or spirit of the nethermost Abyss
Might in that noise reside, of whom to ask
Which way the nearest coast of darkness lies
Bordering on light.

—Paradise Lost

Le jour enfin paraît; et comme les rideaux
d'un tabernacle qu'on relève, des nuages
d'or en s'enroulant à larges volutes
découvrent le ciel.
　　Tout au milieu, et dans le disque
même du soleil, rayonne le face du Jésus-
Christ.[1]

—La Tentation de saint Antoine

A cake of new clean lemon soap arises,
diffusing light and perfume. . . . The
freckled face of Sweny, the druggist,
appears in the disc of the soapsun.

—Ulysses

CHAPTER VI

THE NETHERMOST ABYSS

EXPRESSIONISM IN

LA TENTATION DE SAINT

ANTOINE AND *CIRCE*

$\mathbb{R}$eaders of *Ulysses* generally regard the fifteenth chapter, *Circe*, as the most ambitiously conceived and brilliantly realized episode in the book. Joyce rewrote the chapter from beginning to end nine times, and its composition left him utterly exhausted.[2] Remarking that he intended to send a typescript of *Circe* to Pound, the author went on to reflect wearily, "I do not think that the reading of such a *Walpurgisnacht* will do his or anybody else's health much good."[3] Although most commentators have not shared Joyce's doubts, virtually all of them have conceded the apt-

---

[1] "Day at last appears;—and, like tabernacle curtains uplifted, clouds of gold uprolling in broad volutes unveil the sky."
"Even in the midst thereof, and in the very disk of the sun, beams the face of Jesus Christ." (*The Temptation of St. Anthony*, trans. Lafcadio Hearn [Garden City, N.Y.: Halcyon, n.d.], p. 186. All translated passages are from this edition.)

[2] Cf. *Letters of James Joyce*, ed. Stuart Gilbert and Richard Ellmann (New York, 1957-1966), I, 156.

[3] *Ibid.*, I, 157.

ness of his analogy. Correspondingly, Flaubert's critics have made rapprochements between Goethe's poem and *La Tentation de saint Antoine*. Not only do *Faust* and *Saint Antoine* resemble each other formally, but they also played comparable parts in their authors' lives. The *Tentation* went through three complete versions over a twenty-four-year period; Flaubert spoke of it, with affection and frustration, as the work of a lifetime.[4]

It remained, then, for someone to eliminate the middle term, *Faust*, and to link *Circe* directly with the *Tentation*. Pound did just that in his 1922 review of *Ulysses*, albeit only in passing.[5] Subsequent commentators have reaffirmed the correspondence but likewise without examining it in much depth or detail. Several passages in *Circe* contain obvious allusions to the *Tentation*,[6] but of much greater significance are the broad similarities of theme and form in the two works. In both instances the central action consists in the heroes' becoming the prey of a variety of temptations, fleshly and spiritual. These present themselves in the course of hallucinations induced by fatigue, as well as a lack of food in the saint's case and a surfeit of drink in Stephen's.

---

[4] But consider also Harry Levin's caveat: "To some extent [the *Tentation*] was modelled on *Faust*, which Flaubert had cultivated since his schoolboy discovery of Gérard de Nerval's prose translation. But no distinction could be more strongly marked than that which separates Goethe's archetype of modernity, with his ripening zest for many-sided fulfillment, from the self-mortifying renunciation of Flaubert's emaciated protagonist" (*The Gates of Horn* [New York, 1963], pp. 240-241).

[5] "James Joyce et Pécuchet," *Mercure de France*, CLVI, 315.

[6] Stuart Gilbert, *James Joyce's "Ulysses,"* rev. ed. (New York, 1955), pp. 320-323, quotes several relevant passages from *Ulysses* and the *Tentation*, and I shall deal with others in the course of the chapter.

The structures of the *Tentation* and *Circe* defy ready classification. Neither can be appropriately termed novelistic, although *Circe* performs crucial narrative functions in a book that is a novel among other things. *Saint Antoine* has been described variously as an encyclopedic prose-poem and an expressionist drama.[7] The latter label seems particularly applicable to the more successful features of the work, including those in which Flaubert anticipates Joyce. In Chapter IV we took note of the care and ingenuity with which the two writers rendered mental processes. In the *Tentation* and *Circe* we witness their attempts to probe more deeply into the subjective lives of their characters by dramatically objectifying unconscious and half-conscious fears, desires, and memories. Giving body to these epiphenomena entails radical distortions of time and space. The format Flaubert and Joyce adopt—dialogue and what appear to be stage directions—renders analogies with such theatrical works as Strindberg's *Dream Play* obvious. We have no reason to suppose, however, that either Flaubert or Joyce intended his work to be enacted anywhere except in the mind of the reader, who becomes a spectator in the theatre of his own imagination in much the same way that the protagonists behold their dreams entering on the stage of consciousness from the wings of the psyche.[8]

One respect in which *Circe* differs markedly from the *Tentation* and most other expressionist writings is its atmosphere of relative naturalness. Frank Budgen remarks that "the scene is not the Theban desert or the

---

[7] Cf. Levin, *The Gates of Horn*, pp. 242-243.

[8] *Circe* has, nonetheless, been successfully adapted for the stage by Marjorie Barkentin and Padraic Colum under the title *Ulysses in Nighttown* (New York, 1958). The play was first produced by Burgess Meredith on June 5, 1958, in New York and received highly complimentary reviews.

wild spaces and abysses of the Brocken nor the shifting
scene of a dream, but the common streets of a known
named city and the banal parlour of a cheap brothel.
The persons are not legendary nor are they representative types, but a handful of people of flesh and blood."[9]
Budgen's observation holds so long as we recognize
that Joyce presents the familiar under a fresh aspect,
one that reveals the essential strangeness of much that
seems commonplace. It remains true, however, that not
just the setting and external action of the episode but
the hallucinations themselves have a firm naturalistic
foundation. The visions recapitulate and amplify
themes and events which occur earlier in *Ulysses*; indeed the chapter serves to gather the divergent strands
of the novel together in a climactic finale to the long
central section (Chapters IV through XV) Joyce referred
to as the *Odyssey*.

The fact that the hallucinations in *Circe* are carefully
prepared for gives them a resonance generally lacking
in the *Tentation*, where the scantiness of the narrative
context deprives the saint's visions of some of their
force. Antoine waits passively in the empty desert night
while scenes randomly appear and vanish.[10] Only thematic associations link them in the manner of a dream.

Many of the tableaux that confront the simple hermit—the debate of the heretical sophists or the pantheon
of bizarre deities, for example—lie sufficiently outside
the range of his experience that they cannot be thought
of as issuing from the recesses of his own mind. But
others do seem to have an authentic relation to his
psyche. On several occasions Flaubert anticipates

[9] *James Joyce and the Making of "Ulysses"* (Bloomington,
Ind., 1960), p. 246.

[10] Jean-Pierre Richard, *Littérature et sensation* (Paris, 1954),
p. 153, remarks that "tout arrive au hasard, s'en va de même,
on piétine."

Joyce's practice of allowing a seemingly chance phrase to trigger an elaborate vision.

Early in the *Tentation* a relaxation of Antoine's will leads him to recall his youthful journey with the blind monk Didymus to the unholy city of Alexandria. As a refuge from this distraction, he turns to the Scriptures, but the passages he reads only increase his dissatisfaction with asceticism. One of these texts, Esther 9:5, describes the Maccabees' slaughter of their foes: *"Les Juifs tuèrent tous leurs ennemis avec des glaives et ils en firent un grand carnage, de sorte qu'ils disposèrent à volonté de ceux qu'ils haïssaient."* The saint responds excitedly:

"Suit le dénombrement des gens tués par eux: soixante-quinze mille. Ils avaient tant souffert! D'ailleurs, leurs ennemis étaient les ennemis du vrai Dieu. Et comme ils devaient jouir à se venger, tout en massacrant des idolâtres! La ville, sans doute, regorgeait des morts! Il y en avait au seuil des jardins, sur les escaliers, à une telle hauteur dans les chambres que les portes ne pouvaient plus tourner! . . ."[11]

He terminates this savage revery abruptly when his reason reasserts itself, but his lust for blood and power

[11] *La Tentation de saint Antoine* (Paris: Conard, 1910), p. 9. Subsequent page references will appear in parentheses in the text.

" 'So the Jews made a great slaughter of their enemies with the sword, and killed them, repaying according to what they had prepared to do to them . . .'

"Then comes the number of people slain by them—seventy-five thousand. They had suffered so much! Moreover, their enemies were the enemies of the true God. And how they must have delighted in avenging themselves thus by the massacre of idolaters! Doubtless the city must have been crammed with the dead! There must have been corpses at the thresholds of the garden gates, upon the stairways, in all the chambers, and piled up so high that the doors could no longer move upon their hinges! . . ." (22-23)

and the resentment he feels toward the heterodox and toward those who have not denied themselves as he has are not easily suppressed. A dozen pages later they erupt in an extraordinarily violent fantasy. Meditating on the luxurious splendor of Alexandria, he imagines himself in the midst of an army of monks coming to destroy the Arians:

"Antoine retrouve tous ses ennemis l'un après l'autre. Il en reconnaît qu'il avait oubliés; avant de les tuer, il les outrage. Il éventre, égorge, assomme, traîne les vieillards par la barbe, écrase les enfants, frappe les blessés. Et on se venge du luxe; ceux qui ne savent pas lire déchirent les livres; d'autres cassent, abîment les statues, les peintures, les meubles, les coffrets, mille délicatesses dont ils ignorent l'usage et qui, à cause de cela, les exaspèrent. . . .

"Antoine en a jusqu'aux jarrets. Il marche dedans; il en hume les gouttelettes sur ses lèvres, et tressaille de joie à le sentir contre ses membres, sous sa tunique de poils, qui en est trempée." (23)[12]

The despoliation of Alexandria gives way to another vision, that of the Emperor Constantine's court. Antoine readily acclimates himself to the intrigues of

---

[12] "Anthony finds all his enemies again, one after the other. He even recognizes some whom he had altogether forgotten; before killing them he outrages them. He disembowels—he severs throats—he fells as in a slaughter house—he hales old men by the beard, crushes children, smites the wounded. And vengeance is taken upon luxury, those who do not know how to read tear up books; others smash and deface the statues, paintings, furniture, caskets,—a thousand dainty things the use of which they do not know, and which simply for that reason exasperate them. . . .

"Anthony is up to his knees in it. He wades in it; he sucks up the bloodspray on his lips; he is thrilled with joy as he feels it upon his limbs, under his hair-tunic which is soaked through with it" (36).

political life; the Emperor confides many secrets to him and even asks his advice on matters of health. In the course of his stay the saint notices slaves performing humiliating tasks in the stables. They are the Fathers of the Council of Nicea, whom Constantine detests. When Antoine passes among them, "ils font la haie, le prient d'intercéder, lui baisent les mains. La foule entière les hue; et il jouit de leur dégradation, démesurément. Le voilà devenu un des grands de la Cour, confident de l'Empereur, premier ministre! Constantin lui pose son diadème sur le front. Antoine le garde trouvant cet honneur tout simple" (26).[13]

Even his elevation in rank and the abasement of his rivals prove inadequate to feed Antoine's vanity. Earlier, while he was turning the pages of his Bible, he had come upon Daniel's account of Nebuchadnezzar's bestial self-indulgence and found God's punishment of that king just. Now his dream of Constantinople radiant in the sunlight metamorphoses itself into a vision of Nebuchadnezzar's palace illuminated by golden candelabra. Demoniacal pride, embodied in the King's hedonism and his aspiration to rebuild the Tower of Babel and dethrone God, overwhelms Antoine, who himself becomes Nebuchadnezzar: "Aussitôt il est repu de débordements et d'exterminations, et l'envie le prend de se rouler dans la bassesse. D'ailleurs la dégradation de ce qui épouvante les hommes est un outrage fait à leur esprit, une manière encore de les stupéfier; et comme

---

[13] "They range themselves on either side respectfully; they beseech his intercession; they kiss his hands. The whole assemblage of spectators hoots at them; and he enjoys the spectacle with immeasurable pleasure. Lo! he is now one of the grandees of the Court—the Emperor's confidant—the prime minister! Constantine places his own diadem upon his brows. Anthony allows it to remain upon his head, thinking this honor quite natural" (40).

rien n'est plus vil qu'une bête brute, Antoine se met à quatre pattes sur la table, et beugle comme un taureau" (27).[14]

Finally a pain in the saint's hand—a stone has accidentally wounded him—restores his balance, and he finds himself in front of his hut once again. As a penance for his rebellion, he lashes himself furiously. The self-chastisement is inefficacious, though, for he associates the pain with Ammonaria, a girl whom he knew in his youth and who has become in his imagination an object of desire, and thus he experiences it as pleasure: "Mais voilà qu'un chatouillement me parcourt. Quel supplice! quelles délices! ce sont comme des baisers. Ma moelle se fond! je meurs!" (29)[15] These scenes bear the marks of Flaubert's perennial fascination with the Marquis de Sade, whose fundamental distrust of life he shares.[16]

The interconnection of pain and pleasure, of death and lust, is a major theme in the *Tentation* and one we shall consider at greater length later in this chapter. But for the moment I should like to turn to an episode in *Circe* which offers some striking parallels to the hallucination we have just discussed. In it we find a similar pattern of transformation: Bloom envisions himself as, in turn, a political campaigner, the lord mayor of Dub-

[14] "Immediately he is cloyed with orgiastic excesses, sated with fury of extermination; and a great desire comes upon him to wallow in vileness. For the degradation of that which terrifies men is an outrage inflicted upon their minds—it affords yet one more way to stupefy them; and as nothing is viler than a brute, Anthony goes upon the table on all fours, and bellows like a bull" (41).

[15] "But how strange a titillation thrills me! What punishment! What pleasure! I feel as though receiving invisible kisses; the very marrow of my bones seems to melt. I die . . ." (42-43).

[16] Cf. Benjamin Bart's discussion of sadism in *Salammbô* in his *Flaubert* (Syracuse, N.Y., 1967), pp. 423-426.

lin, the head of state under a variety of titles, and a
spiritual redeemer of sorts. At the end of this sequence
lurks the threat of a loss of humanity comparable to
Antoine's bellowing like a bull. As in the saint's case,
Bloom's need to fulfill his craving for power in dreams
stems in large measure from his actual political impotence. He is indeed isolated from his fellow citizens,
many of whom despise him. Unlike the anchorite,
though, Joyce's hero has little taste for vengeance.

The episode in question is the second of Bloom's hallucinations in *Circe*. In the first his bourgeois conscience arraigns him for committing sundry misdeeds,
whose significance is distorted out of all proportion in
the course of a Kafkaesque trial. Now, as a compensa-
tion, he allows himself to imagine that he is in a position to reconstitute society in accordance with his
ideals. Bloom is engaged in an actual conversation with
an English prostitute, Zoe Higgins. When she asks him
for a cigarette, he tells her, "The mouth can be better
engaged than with a cylinder of rank weed." "Go on,"
Zoe replies sarcastically. "Make a stump speech of it."[17]

Reality dissolves at this point into fantasy. Bloom's
subconscious disregards the sexual pun and fastens on
the denotative meaning of "stump speech." Attired as
a laborer, he declares, "Mankind is incorrigible. . . .
Suicide. Lies. All our habits. Why, look at our public
life!" (478) As if to belie this pessimism, Bloom is
suddenly transformed into the lord mayor of Dublin,
"the world's greatest reformer" (481). In an oration
cast in the diction of nineteenth-century radicalism, he
berates the propertied classes for their faith in machin-
ery and selfish individualism:

"These flying Dutchmen or lying Dutchmen as they

[17] *Ulysses* (New York: Modern Library, 1961), p. 478. Subsequent page references will be incorporated in the text.

recline in their upholstered poop, casting dice, what reck they? Machines is their cry, their chimera, their panacea. Laboursaving apparatuses, supplanters, bugbears, manufactured monsters for mutual murder, hideous hobgoblins produced by a horde of capitalistic lusts upon our prostituted labour. The poor man starves while they are grassing their royal mountain stags or shooting peasants and phartridges in their purblind pomp of pelf and power. But their reign is rover for rever and ever and ev . . ." (479).

The speech is, to be sure, parody, but it still possesses a certain rhetorical force and moral authority. Bloom's critique of industrial society represents an extension of the arguments he has advanced in his debate with the Fenian in Chapter XII, *Cyclops*. The new lord mayor's repudiation of machines as a panacea is somewhat ironic, since all through *Ulysses* he exhibits a fascination with mechanical gadgets and his sole constructive proposal in this episode is to install a tramline from the cattle market to the river. It is true, all the same, that his social position and humanitarian inclinations have never permitted him to exploit his fellows.

The Dubliners are not, in any case, much interested in a continuation of Bloom's polemic, which they drown out with a raucous celebration for their new leader, whom they inaugurate as "undoubted emperor president and king chairman" (482). In his dream, the "competent keyless citizen" (697) receives the keys to the kingdom. In *Cyclops* Bloom has drawn an analogy between the persecution of the Jews and the misfortunes of the Irish.

> —Are you talking about the new Jerusalem? says the citizen.
> —I'm talking about injustice, says Bloom.

—Right, says John Wyse. Stand up to it then with force like men. . . .

—But it's no use, says he. Force, hatred, history, all that. That's not life for men and women, insult and hatred. And everybody knows that it's the very opposite of that that is really life.

—What? says Alf.

—Love, says Bloom. (332-333)

Now, in *Circe*, he promises his subjects that the millennial reign of love is about to dawn: "Yea, on the word of a Bloom, ye shall ere long enter into the golden city which is to be, the new Bloomusalem in the Nova Hibernia of the future" (484). Hailed as the "little father" (486), he dispenses advice on everything from taxes to bladder trouble. Finally the new messiah discloses his program:

"I stand for the reform of municipal morals and the plain ten commandments. New worlds for old. Union of all, jew, moslem and gentile. Three acres and a cow for all children of nature. Saloon motor hearses. Compulsory manual labour for all. All parks open to the public day and night. Electric dishscrubbers. Tuberculosis, lunacy, war and mendicancy must now cease. General amnesty, weekly carnival, with masked licence, bonuses for all, esperanto the universal brotherhood. No more patriotism of barspongers and dropsical imposters. Free money, free love, and a free lay church in a free lay state." (489-490)

Ludicrous as many aspects of this bourgeois utopia appear, and naive as Bloom's turn-of-the-century humanitarian liberalism is, the vitality and good-will which underlie his aspirations are nonetheless admirable. These fundamental attributes remain intact when the fickle mob makes a scapegoat of its "hero god" (492), just as Ireland has betrayed Parnell and all its other champions.

Zoe punctures Bloom's fantasy and returns him to the sordid milieu of the Mecklenburg and Mabbot Street bordellos, where an even keener test than his impulse to messianic materialism awaits him. The danger is that he will shift from an ideal of exaggerated activism to the role of a completely passive victim (whereas his proper station is that of the competent, if keyless, citizen). Like Saint Antoine, Bloom derives sexual pleasure from flagellation.[18] At his imagined trial Mrs. Mervyn Talboys testifies that he has implored her "to bestride and ride him, to give him a most vicious horsewhipping" and expresses her willingness to oblige him. Bloom, quailing expectantly, avows, "I love the danger" (467). Circumstances spare him on this occasion, but later, at Bella Cohen's brothel where he has gone with Zoe, he lapses into another hallucination in which his masochism is given free rein. Confronted by the massive, mustachioed proprietress of the house, he declares, "Exuberant female. Enormously I desiderate your domination" (528). Unmanned, Bloom exchanges sexes with Bella and then sinks down on all fours. Bella, now Bello, "places his heel on her neck and grinds it in" (531) and a moment later gratifies Bloom's urge to be bestridden and ridden:

[18] Richard Ellmann, *James Joyce* (New York, 1959), p. 381, offers a cogent account of the derivation of Bloom's masochistic fantasies from Leopold von Sacher-Masoch's *Venus im Pelz*. He notes, however, two important modifications: "First, his version of Sacher-Masoch is a vaudeville version; and second, Bloom's masochistic fantasies occur in his unconscious mind; he berates himself, and makes himself worse than he is, because he is *conscious* of having allowed too much in reality."

BLOOM

(*Goaded, buttocksmothered.*) O! O! Monsters! Cruel one!

BELLO

Ask for that every ten minutes. Beg, pray for it as you never prayed before. (*He thrusts out a figged fist and foul cigar.*) Here, kiss that. Both. Kiss. (*He throws a leg astride and, pressing with horseman's knees, calls in a hard voice.*) Gee up! A cockhorse to Banbury cross. I'll ride him for the Eclipse stakes. . . . (534)

The comedy of *Circe* grows darker still before Bloom's humiliation is completed. His masochistic fantasies come eventually to center on his cuckoldry; "you have made your secondbest bed," Bello tells him, "and others must lie in it" (543). In one of his visions, Bloom is called upon to witness the rendezvous of Molly and Blazes Boylan that has been in the back of his mind all day. Wearing "a flunkey's plum plush coat and knee-breeches, buff stockings and a powdered wig" (565), he assists at the séance:

MARION

Let him look, the pishogue! Pimp! And scourge himself! I'll write to a powerful prostitute or Bartholomona, the bearded woman, to raise weals out on him an inch thick and make him bring me back a signed and stamped receipt.

BELLA

(*Laughing.*) Ho ho ho ho.

BOYLAN

(*To Bloom, over his shoulder.*) You can apply your eye to the keyhole and play with yourself while I just go through her a few times.

BLOOM

Thank you, sir, I will, sir. May I bring two men
chums to witness the deed and take a snapshot?
(*He holds an ointment jar.*) Vaseline, sir? Orange-
flower? . . . Lukewarm water? . . . (566)

Joyce's practice in *Circe* is, as I have indicated, to
draw the matter of Bloom's and Stephen's hallucinations from thoughts and experiences each character
has had earlier in the day. The most conspicuous exception occurs at this point in the chapter: "Stephen
and Bloom gaze in the mirror. The face of William
Shakespeare, beardless, appears there, rigid in facial
paralysis, crowned by the reflection of the reindeer
antlered hatrack in the hall" (567). The cuckold's
horns are certainly apposite to Bloom's condition, but
it is Stephen who, in *Scylla and Charybdis*, has elab-
orated a theory that the author of *Hamlet* was a de-
ceived husband. A moment later Stephen sees "the face
of Martin Cunningham, bearded, refeatur[ing] Shakespeare's beardless face" (568), although it is Bloom
who, at Glasnevin cemetery, has associated Cunningham's sympathetic, intelligent aspect with Shakespeare's (96). This psychic sharing underscores the
possibilities for communion between Leopold and Stephen, possibilities which, for the former at least, come
to seem worth cultivating as the episode progresses.

One should not infer that Molly's role in *Circe* consists only in revealing her husband's voyeurism and
latent masochism. Throughout *Ulysses* Molly, who is
half-Spanish, symbolizes the erotic vibrancy of Medi-
terranean lands. Early in the chapter she appears before him clad in Turkish costume and standing by "her
mirage of datepalms" (439):

"Beside her a camel, hooded with a turreting turban,
waits. A silk ladder of innumerable rungs climbs to

his bobbing howdah. He ambles near with disgruntled hindquarters. Fiercely she slaps his haunch, her gold-curb wristbangles angriling, scolding him in Moorish. ... The camel, lifting a foreleg, plucks from a tree a large mango fruit, offers it to his mistress, blinking, in his cloven hoof, then droops his head and, grunting, with uplifted neck, fumbles to kneel. Bloom stoops his back for leapfrog." (439-440)

Let us compare a parallel passage in the *Tentation*:

"Un éléphant blanc, caparaçonné d'un filet d'or, accourt, en secouant le bouquet de plumes d'autruche attaché à son frontal.

"Sur son dos, parmi des coussins de laine bleue, jambes croisées, paupières à demi closes et se balançant la tête, il y a une femme si splendidement vêtue qu'elle envoie des rayons autour d'elle. La foule se prosterne, l'éléphant plie les genoux, et

LA REINE DE SABA,

se laissant glisser le long de son épaule, descend sur le tapis et s'avance vers saint Antoine." (29)[19]

Molly Bloom and the Queen of Sheba have in common a Circean capacity for reducing men to the status of the submissive animals that attend them. That Molly is satisfied with Bloom's camel-like obsequious-

---

[19] "A white elephant, caparisoned with a golden net, trots forward, shaking the tuft of ostrich plumes attached to his head-band.

"Upon his back, perched on cushions of blue wool, with her legs crossed, her eyes half closed, her comely head sleepily nodding, is a woman so splendidly clad that she radiates light about her. The crowd falls prostrate; the elephant bends his knees; and

THE QUEEN OF SHEBA

letting herself glide down from his shoulder upon the carpets spread to receive her, approaches Saint Anthony" (43).

Gilbert (p. 321) points out the similarity between this passage and the one in *Circe*, but he does not develop the implications of the correspondence.

ness, his offer to serve in Boylan's stead as her "business menagerer," seems doubtful, for she advises him to "go and see life. See the wide world" (440). Her feminine charms constitute both a means of dominating her husband and a powerful inducement to him to resume his proper role as master in his own house. In the latter case it is not a temptation she offers but a challenge.

Antoine, on the other hand, has a religious commitment to remain poor, chaste, and obedient to an austere discipline. The Queen of Sheba comes bearing an invitation to partake of her riches, her body, and her hedonistic values. The test is a severe one for the saint, suffering from years of deprivation. When the Queen commands him to behold her eyes, darker than mystic caverns, he does so in spite of himself. "Toutes celles que tu as rencontrées, depuis la fille des carrefours chantant sous sa lanterne jusqu'à la patricienne effeuillant des roses du haut de sa litière, toutes les formes entrevues, toutes les imaginations de ton désir, demandeles!" she tells Antoine. "Je ne suis pas une femme, je suis un monde!" (36)[20] Even these Cleopatra-like attractions are insufficient, though, to bring about his capitulation; the saint has renounced the world, and when the Queen departs, "en poussant une sorte de hoquet convulsif, qui ressemble à des sanglots ou à un ricanement" (37),[21] he seems to consider her a world well lost.

[20] "All the women thou hast ever met—from the leman of the cross-roads, singing under the light of her lantern, even to the patrician lady scattering rose-petals abroad from her litter,—all the forms thou hast ever obtained glimpses of—all the imaginations of thy desire thou hast only to ask for them! I am not a woman: I am a world!" (51)

[21] "The Queen of Sheba departs, uttering a convulsive hiccough at intervals, which might be taken either for a sound of

For Flaubert debauchery and death are inseparable, and, as Levin notes, "his fondest antitheses are those that wed the carnal to the charnel."[22] In the seventh section of the *Tentation*, Antoine recalls nostalgically having amused himself as a child by constructing hermitages out of pebbles while his mother looked on. But this serene remembrance quickly dissipates when he reflects that she opposed his becoming an archorite: "Elle m'aura maudit pour mon abandon, en arrachant à pleines mains ses cheveux blancs. Et son cadavre est resté étendu au milieu de la cabane, sous le toit de roseaux, entre les murs qui tombent. Par un trou, une hyène en reniflant, avance la gueule!" (179)[23]

The saint attempts to assuage his conscience by speculating that Ammonaria has stayed with his mother. He succeeds, however, only in conjuring up an image of his childhood companion that quickens his desire and adds to his perplexity: "Voilà ma chair qui se révolte!" he cries out. "Au milieu du chagrin la concupiscence me torture. Deux supplices à la fois, c'est trop! Je ne peux plus endurer ma personne!" (180)[24] And he meditates on the ease with which he could put his cares to rest, simply by rolling off the precipice on which he is perched. The one recurrent temptation which menaces Antoine most gravely is that of yield-

---

hysterical sobbing, or the half-suppressed laughter of mockery" (52).

[22] *The Gates of Horn*, p. 242.

[23] "Will she not have cursed me for having abandoned her? —Will she not have plucked out her white hair by handfuls in the despair of her grief? And her corpse remains lying on the floor of the hut, under the roof of reeds, between the crumbling walls. Through an orifice a hyena, sniffing, thrusts his head, advances his mouth!" (166)

[24] "What! my flesh rebels again! Even in the midst of grief am I tortured by concupiscence. To be subjected thus unto two tortures at once is beyond endurance! I can no longer bear myself!" (166)

ing to despair. Were he to become a suicide he would have committed not only an irrevocable act but, within the Christian context he inhabits, an irremissible sin. The moment is ripe, then, for one of the climactic visions of the *Tentation*.

An old woman resembling his mother appears before the saint and, appealing to his pride, urges him to take his life: "Faire une chose qui vous égale à Dieu, pense donc! Il t'a créé, tu vas détruire son oeuvre, toi, par ton courage, librement!" (181) Her arguments are countered by a beautiful young woman, whom the hermit at first takes to be Ammonaria and who counsels, "Vis donc, jouis donc! Salomon recommande la joie! Va comme ton coeur te mène et selon le désir de tes yeux!" (182)[25] The shroud cloaking the old woman and the young woman's dress split open and the two disclose their true identities: they are Death and Lechery. Their contest for Antoine's soul continues, the former glorying in the joys of destruction and the latter emphasizing the cold terror at the core of sensual delight, until each recognizes in the other her sister:

LA LUXURE

Ma colère vaut la tienne. Je hurle, je mords. J'ai des sueurs d'agonisant et des aspects de cadavre.

LA MORT

C'est moi qui te rends sérieuse; enlaçons-nous! *La Mort ricane, la Luxure rugit. Elles se prennent par la taille, et chantent ensemble:*

[25] "To do that which will make thee equal unto God—think! He created thee: thou wilt destroy his work—thou! and by thy courage,—of thy own free will!" (167)
"Nay, live! enjoy! Solomon counsels joy! Follow the guiding of thy heart and the desire of thine eyes!" (168)

—Je hâte la dissolution de la matière!
—Je facilite l'éparpillement des germes!
—Tu détruis, pour mes renouvellements!
—Tu engendres, pour mes destructions!
—Active ma puissance!
—Féconde ma pourriture! (186)[26]

Saint Antoine sees them as the Devil in his twofold aspect and declares that neither frightens him. "Je repousse le bonheur, et je me sens éternel," he avows. "Ainsi la mort n'est qu'une illusion, un voile masquant par endroits la continuité de la vie" (187).[27] As the reader might suspect, the triumph of faith proves as transient in this instance as in all those which have preceded it, but that is a matter we must leave until the end of the chapter.

The very different attitudes on the part of Bloom and Stephen toward mortality that we observed in the *Proteus* and *Hades* episodes are evident once again in *Circe*. Stephen's sense of guilt at his mother's death comes to the surface in a form that vividly recalls Antoine's vision of *his* mother's corpse. Stephen, Lynch, Bloom, and the whores have been dancing to the music of the pianola when Stephen's father, Simon Dedalus,

[26] "LUST. 'My rage equals thine! I also yell; I bite! I, too, have sweats of agony, and aspects cadaverous!'
"DEATH. 'It is I that make thee awful! Let us intertwine!'
"(*Death laughs mockingly; Lust roars. They clasp each other about the waist, and chant alternately*):
" 'I hasten the dissolution of matter!'
" 'I facilitate the dispersion of germs!'
" 'Thou dost destroy for my renovations!'
" 'Thou dost engender for my destructions!'
" 'Ever-active my power!'
" 'Fecund, my putrefaction!' " (173)
[27] "I repel happiness; and I know myself to be eternal."
"Thus death is only an illusion, a veil masking betimes the continuity of life" (173).

suddenly appears and admonishes, "Think of your mother's people!" "Dance of death," (579) replies the son. An instant later the *danse macabre* halts as "Stephen's mother, emaciated, rises stark through the floor in leper grey with a wreath of faded orange blossoms and a torn bridal veil, her face worn and noseless, green with grave mould. Her hair is scant and lank. She fixes her bluecircled hollow eyesockets on Stephen and opens her toothless mouth, uttering a silent word" (579).

Stephen, choking with horror and remorse, denies responsibility for her condition: "They said I killed you, mother. . . . Cancer did it, not I" (580). Then, as his initial fright lessens, eschatological curiosity gets the better of him and he asks eagerly that she tell him "the word known to all men" (581). Even in death, however, she remains a simple, conventionally pious woman who can say, in the same breath, "I pray for you in my other world. Get Dilly to make you that boiled rice every night after your brain work" (581). But the real aim of her hallucinatory visitation is to win Stephen away from his rebellion against the church.

THE MOTHER

(*Her face drawing near and nearer, sending out an ashen breath.*) Beware! (*She raises her blackened, withered right arm slowly towards Stephen's breast with outstretched fingers.*) Beware! God's hand! (*A green crab with malignant red eyes sticks deep its grinning claws in Stephen's heart.*)

STEPHEN

(*Strangled with rage.*) Shite! (*His features grow drawn and grey and old.*)

BLOOM

(*At the window.*) What?

STEPHEN

Ah non, par exemple! The intellectual imagination!
With me all or not at all. *Non serviam!* (582)

Stephen's continued defiance represents a defense
of his integrity that is in some respects parallel to Saint
Antoine's jousting with the Devil. It differs, though, in
that Joyce stands at a greater distance from the young
man than does Flaubert from his protagonist; Stephen's
refusal to submit to the crabbed hand of God is depicted
comically. Echoing Siegfried's cry—"*Nothung!*"—"he
lifts his ashplant high with both hands and smashes
the chandelier. Time's livid final flame leaps and, in
the following darkness, ruin of all space, shattered glass
and toppling masonry" (583). What has actually oc-
curred, we discover subsequently, is less cosmic in its
implications than the preceding description indicates:
Stephen has broken the chimney of one of Bella Cohen's
lamps and dented its shade. The juxtaposition of in-
tense and trivial feelings within the vision and the
counterpointing of the vision itself with the banal circumstances in which it takes place point up the essential irrationality of the fears Stephen retains as a result
of his Jesuit education.

Joyce discounts Stephen's attitude toward death even
more effectively by contrasting it with Bloom's. The
latter is visited not only by his deceased parents, who
reproach him for being imprudent, but by his grand-
father, Lipoti Virag, who "chutes rapidly down through
the chimneyflue" (511). The "basilico-grammate" carries a roll of parchment under several overcoats and
has a quill behind each ear. Virag's droll appearance
suggests the immense gap between Bloom's sympathetic
openness to influence from the past and Stephen's mor-
bid dread of what he has described as "a nightmare
from which I am trying to awake" (34).

When Virag arrives on the scene, he finds his grandson smiling desirously at the prostitutes, twirling his thumbs. The old scholar offers shrewd, humorous analyses of the three whores' shortcomings to which Leopold is obliged to give assent. "Stop twirling your thumbs and have a good old thunk," Virag admonishes, "Exercise your mnemotechnic" (514). His warnings serve to remind Bloom of the moral tradition to which he belongs. "In a moment of vision," points out S. L. Goldberg, "he sees himself as he was by the light of what he now is and what in possibility he may come to be. . . . The tradition of rational, critical detachment, represented by the weird, dispossessed ghost of Virag, enables Bloom to disengage himself from lust."[28] And this capacity for dispassionate reflection allows the latter to perceive what Stephen cannot: "The touch of a deadhand cures" (514).

Frank Budgen discerns a precedent for the self-critical *alter ego* personified as Lipoti Virag in Hilarion, the former pupil of Saint Antoine who returns in the anchorite's dreams to dissect his motives.[29] Like Virag, Hilarion possesses a keen intellect and a faculty for penetrating psychological analysis. In a moment of scathing candor, he exclaims,

"Hypocrite qui s'enfonce dans la solitude pour se livrer mieux au débordement de ses convoitises! Tu te prives de viandes, de vin, d'étuves, d'esclaves et d'honneurs; mais comme tu laisses ton imagination t'offrir des banquets, des parfums, des femmes nues et des foules applaudissantes! Ta chasteté n'est qu'une corruption plus subtile, et ce mépris du monde l'impuissance de ta haine contre lui!" (42)[30]

---

[28] *The Classical Temper* (London, 1961), p. 182.
[29] *James Joyce and the Making of "Ulysses,"* p. 239.
[30] "Hypocrite! burying thyself in solitude only in order the more fully to abandon thyself to the indulgence of thy envious

Hilarion does not, however, share Virag's fundamental sympathy for the hero. He is revealed finally as an allegorical figure for Science, the most modern guise of Antoine's antagonist, the Devil.

Initially the hermit regards his disciple under a very different aspect. Musing on the boy's appealing character, he remarks, "C'était un fils pour moi!" (5) And indeed at his advent in the *Tentation* Hilarion does assume the form of a child, albeit a singularly unattractive one: "Cet enfant est petit comme un nain, et pourtant trapu comme un Cabire, contourné, d'aspect misérable. Des cheveux blancs couvrent sa tête prodigieusement grosse; et il grelotte sous une méchante tunique, tout en gardant à sa main un rouleau de papyrus" (38).[31] Thus his appearance is hardly a consolation for the tormented saint, nor is it calculated to gratify any suppressed paternal longings he may experience.

The search for a son is, in any case, a much more prominent theme in *Ulysses*. Throughout the novel Bloom seeks a social role in which his impulse to love can express itself fully and finds himself frustrated at almost every turn. If Dublin seems to deny him that opportunity, it at least furnishes a young man whose art may some day create a just image of Bloom's ben-

---

desires! What if thou dost deprive thyself of meats, of wine, of warmth, of bath, of slaves, of honours?—dost thou not permit thy imagination to offer thee banquets, perfumes, women, and the applause of multitudes? Thy chastity is but a more subtle form of corruption, and thy contempt of this world is but the impotence of thy hatred against it!" (55)

[31] "He was a son to me (19)."

"This child is small like a dwarf, and nevertheless squat of build, like one of the Cabiri; deformed withal, and wretched of aspect. His prodigiously large head is covered with white hair; and he shivers under a shabby tunic, all the while clutching a roll of papyrus" (53).

evolence for men to behold. (Does not *Ulysses* itself accomplish precisely that?) Stephen, at this point a homeless inebriate, very much needs the older man's guidance and protection. Chance, in the form of a button popping off his trousers, intervenes to restore Bloom's self-possession. He takes custody of Stephen's meagre funds, tries to prevent him from brawling with two English soldiers, keeps him out of the hands of the watch, and finally offers him a refuge for the night.

At the close of *Circe*, Bloom "stands on guard, his fingers at his lips in the attitude of a secret master" (609). The rites of freemasonry are emblematic of the "mystical estate" (207) of fatherhood, the relation in which he now stands to Stephen. We need scarcely wonder why the sight of Stephen's prostrate form evokes in the older man's mind a vision of his own son Rudy, who died in infancy: "Against the dark wall a figure appears slowly, a fairy boy of eleven, a changeling, kidnapped, dressed in an Eton suit with glass shoes and a little bronze helmet, holding a book in his hand. He reads from right to left inaudibly, smiling, kissing the page" (609).[32] Despite his sentimental view

---

[32] A curious parallel occurs in *L'Education sentimentale* (Paris, 1910), p. 516, when Rosanette Bron informs Frédéric that she is pregnant with his child: "L'idée d'être père . . . lui paraissait grotesque, inadmissible. Mais pourquoi? Si, au lieu de la Maréchale. . . ? Et sa rêverie devint tellement profonde, qu'il eut une sorte d'hallucination. Il voyait là, sur le tapis, devant la cheminée, une petite fille. Elle ressemblait à Mme Arnoux et à lui-même, un peu; brune et blanche, avec des yeux noirs, de très grands sourcils, un ruban rose dans ses cheveux bouclants! Oh! comme il l'aurait aimée! Et il lui semblait entendre sa voix: 'Papa: papa!'"/ "The idea of being a father struck him as grotesque, unthinkable. But why should it? If, instead of the Marshal. . . . ? And he became so absorbed in his reverie that he had a sort of hallucination. There on the carpet in front of the fireplace, he saw a little girl. She took after Madame Arnoux and a little after him: dark-haired and pale-skinned, with black eyes, thick eyebrows, and a pink rib-

of childhood, Bloom's recognition that he has something of value to bestow on a son—"I could have helped
him on in life" (89)—is apposite to his tie with Stephen.
He alone has a sense of the young man's potentialities.
And the perpetuation of his heritage, if it is to occur
at all, requires as its vehicle an adopted son. As Bloom
has said regarding Queen Victoria, "her son was the
substance. Something new to hope for not like the
past she wanted back, waiting" (101).

The kindness and balanced judgment that are the
principal gifts Bloom could offer a son are rooted deeply
in his humanism. Saint Antoine's life is, of course,
grounded on a radically divergent principle: his ultimate hope lies in communion with the Son of Man.
When the sun rises, ending the dark night of Antoine's
soul, the hermit sees

> des nuages d'or en s'enroulant à larges volutes
> découvrent le ciel.
>
> Tout au milieu, et dans le disque même du soleil,
> rayonne la face de Jésus-Christ.
>
> Antoine fait le signe de la croix et se remet en
> prières. (201)[33]

Whether this conclusion implies that "il a reçu la
grâce, don merveilleux, gratuit,"[34] remains open to
question. What emerges much more clearly is the
steadfastness that the saint shares with Leopold Bloom.

---

bon in her curly hair. Oh, how he would have loved her! And
he seemed to hear her voice calling: 'Papa! papa!'" (*Sentimental Education*, trans. Robert Baldick [Baltimore, 1964], pp.
355-356.)

[33] "Clouds of gold uprolling in broad volutes unveil the sky."
"Even in the midst thereof, and in the very disk of the sun,
beams the face of Jesus Christ."
"Anthony makes the sign of the cross, and resumes his devo-
tions." (186)

[34] Alfred Colling, *Gustave Flaubert* (Paris, 1941), p. 315.

CHAPTER VII

IMPASSIVE STARS

THE VISION OF FACT
IN *BOUVARD ET PÉCUCHET*
AND *ITHACA*

Le silence éternel de ces espaces
infinis m'effraie.[1]

—PASCAL

Il y'avait entre ces clartés de
grands espaces vides, et le firmament
semblait une mer d'azur, avec
des archipels et des îlots.
    —Quelle quantité! s'écria Bouvard.
. . . C'est à rendre fou. . . .
    Ils parlaient ainsi, debout sur le
vigneau, à la lueur des astres, et
leur discours était coupé par de
longs silences.[2]

—Bouvard et Pécuchet

Alone, what did Bloom feel?
    The cold of interstellar space,
thousands of degrees below freezing
point or the absolute zero of
Fahrenheit, Centigrade or Réaumur
. . . the apathy of the stars.

—Ulysses

CHAPTER VII

IMPASSIVE STARS

THE VISION OF FACT

IN *BOUVARD ET PÉCUCHET*

AND *ITHACA*

Seeking a literary precedent which would help French readers come to terms with *Ulysses*, Ezra Pound fixed on Flaubert's last work, *Bouvard et Pécuchet*. The latter, he maintained, had inaugurated a new form and one which no subsequent fiction writer except Joyce had dared to employ: an anatomy of universal imbecility, with "l'homme-type," the most general of generalizations, at its center. Besides Joyce, "only Rabelais and Flaubert attacked a whole century."[3]

[1] "The eternal silence of these infinite spaces frightens me."

[2] "Between these lights there were vast empty spaces, and the firmament appeared to be a sea of blue, with archipelagos and islands.

" 'What a lot of them!' cried Bouvard. . . . 'It's enough to drive one mad!'

"They spoke in this fashion, posted on the mound, in the starlight, and their conversation was divided by long silences." (*Bouvard and Pécuchet*, trans. T. W. Earp and G. W. Stonier [Norfolk, Conn.: New Directions, 1954], pp. 93-94. All translated passages are from this edition.)

[3] "James Joyce et Pécuchet," *Mercure de France*, CLVI (June

Many, perhaps most, readers would take exception to Pound's claim that the authors' attitudes toward their characters are fundamentally the same and the protagonists themselves no more than bourgeois versions of everyman. We should have to agree, of course, that criticism of a civilization addicted to *idées reçues*, fashionable opinions held uncritically, is an important element in the two books. For most of us, though, the satire of what T. S. Eliot, in another early review of *Ulysses*, called "the immense panorama of futility and anarchy which is contemporary history"[4] is not the center of interest in either novel. Literary critiques of bourgeois life are common enough, and the reputations of Flaubert and Joyce hardly rest on their originality as social thinkers. When we do encounter profound psychological or sociological insights in their works, these almost always seem to have been generated by the pressure of imaginative composition rather than to have resulted from abstract speculation. As Flaubert himself remarked to George Sand, "I try to think well in order to write well. But my aim is to write well—I have never said it was anything else."[5] What matters most, then, is not the two novelists' choice of "sub-literary" subjects nor even the tone they adopt toward them but rather the formal means by which they turned these materials to artistic account.

Flaubert intended to provide in *Bouvard et Pécuchet* a *reductio ad absurdum* of a massive slice of French

---

1, 1922), 316. "Entre 1880 et l'année où fut commencé *Ulysses* personne n'a eu le courage de faire le sottisier gigantesque, ni la patience de rechercher l'homme-type, la généralisation la plus générale" (312).

[4] "Ulysses, Order and Myth," in *James Joyce: Two Decades of Criticism*, ed. Seon Givens (New York, 1948), p. 201.

[5] *The Selected Letters of Gustave Flaubert*, trans. and ed. Francis Steegmuller (New York, 1953), p. 251 (*Correspondance* [Paris: Conard, 1926-1933], VII, 282).

cultural life. Naturally this aim presented imposing technical difficulties, the first of them being the selection of a suitable framework. The answer to this problem he found in the efforts of the eighteenth-century *philosophes* to give a semblance of order to the polymorphous mass of data which the new learning had heaped against the walls of their studies.[6] *Bouvard et Pécuchet* was to follow their lead, then, and become a kind of encyclopedia—*une encyclopédie mise en farce.* Abandonment of the spurious claim to integration encyclopedists make, alphabetic arrangement of their shards of information, would disclose the chaotic nature of the bourgeois mind, which reduces all subjects to a common level of inanity. One finds a comparable flattening of perspective in *Ithaca,* the seventeenth chapter of *Ulysses* and the one that most closely resembles Flaubert's last book. Its sheer weight of language and unchanging tempo seem to imply that everything recounted is of equal significance.

Mechanical gracelessness and incongruity are, of course, classic ingredients of humor, but on the scale that encyclopedias manifest these attributes, they are more often a source of tedium than laughter. Any comedy which takes encyclopedism as its method demands extraordinary patience on the part of its audi-

[6] Cf. Hugh Kenner, *Flaubert, Joyce and Beckett: The Stoic Comedians* (Boston, 1962), pp. 1-2: "The Encyclopaedia, like its cousin the Dictionary, takes all that we know apart into little pieces, and then arranges those pieces so that they can be found one at a time. It is produced by a feat of organizing, not a feat of understanding. . . . If the Encyclopaedia means anything as a whole, no one connected with the enterprise can be expected to know what that meaning is. . . . That the great *Encyclopédie* contained cross-references to articles which did not exist is not surprising under the circumstances, nor is the presence of wholesale contradiction within the covers of any such bound set; nor, finally, the nearly surrealist discontinuity of the final product."

ence, and whatever satisfaction it offers is bound to entail considerable cerebration rather than the sort of spontaneous enjoyment one generally associates with humor. The impression of sameness over many pages is an effect novelists traditionally have sought to avoid, if for no other reason than that readers find it tiresome. Only with the rise of the *nouveau roman* has boring one's public enjoyed any wide acceptance as a legitimate aim of fiction; Flaubert and Joyce stand as precursors of this new mode in their efforts to achieve an artistically brilliant kind of monotony. Anthony Thorlby calls attention to the rigorous demands placed on Flaubert's stylistic virtuosity:

"Each fact is isolated in turn, with sufficient detachment from the next to emphasize the absence of any real perspective between one kind of fact and another. And since facts presented all from the same point of view inevitably fall into some kind of perspective and assume a real meaning as a whole, this has required a constant interruption of stylistic continuity, by means of every change in tense, person, subject, tone, direct and reported speech, and whatever other device of syntax and vocabulary Flaubert could muster. That is why virtually every phrase set him a new problem in expression: how to turn it aesthetically to bring out its essential sameness as fact."[7]

This analysis adheres to requirements of comedy the novelist himself sets forth: "Il faut disloquer la phrase, souligner les mots, peser les syllabes."[8]

Perhaps the most obvious instances of this inten-

[7] *Gustave Flaubert and the Art of Realism* (London, 1956), pp. 54-55.

[8] *Bouvard et Pécuchet* (Paris: Conard, 1910), p. 171. Subsequent page references will appear in parentheses in the text.

"Every phrase must be pulled to pieces, every word underlined, every syllable weighed" (155).

tionally disjointed prose in *Bouvard et Pécuchet* are the
many inventories of the characters' possessions, attitudes, and experiences. The catalogue of the contents
of Pécuchet's room on the Rue Saint-Martin, which appears in Chapter I, will serve as an example: "Un bu-
reau de sapin, placé juste dans le milieu, incommodait
par ses angles; et tout autour, sur des planchettes, sur
les trois chaises, sur le vieux fauteuil et dans les coins
se trouvaient pêle-mêle plusieurs volumes de l'*Encyclopédie Roret*, le *Manuel du magnétiseur*, un Fénelon,
d'autres bouquins, avec des tas de paperasses, deux
noix de coco, diverses médailles, un bonnet turc et des
coquilles rapportées du Havre par Dumouchel" (6-7).[9]
Pécuchet's belongings are actually not so inconse-
quential as this listing makes them appear, for they
adumbrate the accumulation of junk we see later in
the "museum" at Chavignolles and the books, especially
the *Roret*, form the nucleus of what comes to be a siza-
ble, if somewhat eccentric, collection.

Joyce relies even more heavily on the inventory device. Bloom's library, numbering twenty-odd volumes
(among them such items as *Thom's Dublin Post Of-
fice Directory* and several popular handbooks of astronomy), is described in sufficient detail—including the
nature and position of bookmarks—to satisfy the most
ardent bibliographer. Household goods too are meticu-
lously catalogued. When Bloom enters the front room
at 7 Eccles Street, he discovers that someone has re-

[9] "A deal table, set exactly in the middle of the room, was
always in the way with its corners; and round it, on the little
tables, the three chairs, the old arm-chair, and in the corners,
were scattered a number of volumes of the Roret Encyclopaedia, the Mesmerist's Handbook, a Fénelon, and other old tomes,
as well as a pile of papers, two coconuts, various medallions,
a Turkish fez, and shells brought from Havre by Dumouchel"
(21).

arranged the furniture. A third of a page is devoted to an account of the four changes that have been made and another two-thirds to a minute examination of several of the articles involved. One of them is "a squat stuffed easychair with stout arms extended and back slanted to the rere, which, repelled in recoil, had then upturned an irregular fringe of a rectangular rug and now displayed on its amply upholstered seat a centralised diffusing and diminishing discolouration."[10] An equally detailed description of its mate follows. Lest anyone think this sort of verbal upholstery unwarranted, Joyce furnishes an explicit justification:

"What significances attached to these two chairs?

"Significances of similitude, of posture, of symbolism, of circumstantial evidence, of testimonial supermanence." (706)

This bit of pedantic whimsy is, of course, a pulling of the reader's leg; all the same, many of the prosaic objects appearing in *Ithaca*, such as the door key Bloom has forgotten to put in his pocket or the crumbs of potted meat he finds in his bed, do carry a symbolic charge—a matter to which we shall return later in the chapter. Our immediate concern is with Joyce's style, a style which in this episode deranges normal syntax and throws words into isolation. Neologisms occur almost as frequently as they do in *Finnegans Wake*, and indeed the later chapters of *Ulysses* point clearly toward the linguistic inventiveness of Joyce's final work. This prose, with its abstract and grotesque diction and its cacophonous rhythms, has, as Stanley Sultan says, "a fresh, albeit precious, charm, the charm of harmonious unfailing wrongness."[11] Joyce himself

[10] *Ulysses* (New York: Modern Library, 1961), p. 706. Subsequent page references will be incorporated in the text.

[11] *The Argument of "Ulysses"* (Columbus, Ohio, 1964), p. 382.

considered *Ithaca,* "the ugly duckling of the book," his favorite episode.[12]

"I am writing *Ithaca,*" he told Budgen, "in the form of a mathematical catechism. All events are resolved into their cosmic, physical, psychical, etc. equivalents . . . so that the reader will know everything and know it in the baldest and coldest way, but Bloom and Stephen thereby become heavenly bodies, wanderers like the stars at which they gaze."[13] The last clause seems more than just a fillip; it implies that Joyce's "bald" treatment of his material does not entail a repudiation of the protagonists, even though it increases the distance between himself and the two of them. His portrayal of the sensibility of urban man, choking on the detritus of technological civilization, embraces his heroes, Bloom in particular, but they still manage to come through the episode as something more than vacuous *hommes-types.* The final effect of Joyce's critical irony is "not to demolish Bloom and Stephen into scattered, fragmentary 'facts,' but rather to show their invulnerability to this view of them," Goldberg rightly asserts. "The artist's assumption of an absurdly cold, implacable superiority (which is always parodying itself) is meant to recall to us, by reaction, the artist's continual activity *within* his creation. Taken in the total context of the work, it parodies the method and outlook of naturalistic Realism in order to suggest what lies beyond its grasp."[14]

Joyce devotes the first half of *Ithaca* to plotting the "parallel courses" Bloom and Stephen follow. The third

---

[12] Frank Budgen, *James Joyce and the Making of "Ulysses"* (Bloomington, Ind., 1960), p. 258.

[13] *Letters of James Joyce,* ed. Stuart Gilbert and Richard Ellmann (New York, 1957-1966), I, 159-160.

[14] *The Classical Temper* (London, 1961), pp. 189-190.

question in the catechism outlines several affinities
which might serve to bring them closer to each other:
"Both were sensitive to artistic impressions musical in
preference to plastic or pictorial. Both preferred a con-
tinental to an insular manner of life, a cisatlantic to a
transatlantic place of residence. Both indurated by early domestic training and an inherited tenacity of heterodox resistance professed their disbelief in many ortho-
dox religious, national, social and ethical doctrines.
Both admitted the alternately stimulating and obtund-
ing influence of heterosexual magnetism" (666). Cos-
mopolitanism, nonconformity, and heterosexuality are
dispositions the author shares with his protagonists and
means, presumably, to endorse. Of these, their response
to "heterosexual magnetism" appears most fundamental, for in the course of this episode they draw ever
nearer to Molly Bloom, the embodiment of *das Ewig-
Weibliche*. In Molly there is neither Greek, nor Jew,
nor Irish Catholic; she cares little or nothing about
artistic preferences, political loyalties, or religious be-
liefs, and the similarities and differences in the intellectual make-up of Stephen and her husband pale into
insignificance as we become aware of her presence. Her
life-giving power provides a ground on which two men
can meet and establish some measure of communion.
Bloom is fully conscious of the force she incarnates,
and there are signs that Stephen is beginning to awaken
to it as well. The first object of any importance that
Stephen notices upon entering the house on Eccles
Street is Molly's hose.

The fore part of *Ithaca* focuses on the question of
whether these two Dubliners can indeed surmount the
factors that divide them—differences of race, creed,
ancestry, and experience. The alternative explanations
they offer for Stephen's collapse outside Bella Cohen's

brothel, though seemingly trivial, reveal a significant divergence of temperament. Bloom, the matter-of-fact bourgeois, ascribes it to an excess of alcohol and "the rapid circular motion" of Private Carr's fist. Stephen, the would-be artist, attributes his fall to the "reapparition of a matutinal cloud . . . at first no bigger than a woman's hand" (667). The substitution of "woman" for "man" in this allusion to I Kings 18:44 is yet another outcropping of Stephen's sense of responsibility for his mother's death and further evidence of his continuing estrangement from the eternal feminine. Their perceptions underscore a parallactic disparity of vision: Stephen's prostration and the appearance of the cloud that morning have been, like so many other events in the book, "perceived by both from two different points of observation" (667). Can their parallel courses ever defy the circumstances that define them and converge?

There is no clear answer. Bloom takes the initiative and finds Stephen, for the most part, insensitive to his overtures. The latter declines to stay for the night, and the older man recognizes that the chances of their meeting again are slight. Before Stephen's departure, though, a few moments of genuine rapport do exist. The despondency Bloom feels in the face of formidable barriers to human fulfillment—"the painful character of the ultimate functions of separate existence"—leads him to "desist from speculation . . . because it was a task for a superior intelligence to substitute other more acceptable phenomena in place of the less acceptable phenomena" (697). As it happens, a "superior intelligence," one capable of articulating what Bloom cannot, is at hand.

Did Stephen participate in his dejection? He affirmed his significance as a conscious rational

animal proceeding syllogistically from the known
to the unknown and a conscious rational reagent
between a micro- and a macrocosm ineluctably
constructed upon the incertitude of the void.
Was this affirmation apprehended by Bloom?
Not verbally. Substantially.
What comforted his misapprehension?
That as a competent keyless citizen he had pro-
ceeded energetically from the unknown to the
known through the incertitude of the void. (697)

Closer than that the two men cannot, on the naturalistic plane of the book, come. Their disparate personalities can be reconciled, if at all, only through a long
process of adjustment on Stephen's part, and a few
hours of their lives are all we are allowed to witness.
What is impossible on the realistic level, though, may
be dealt with on the symbolic; indeed, Joyce plays out
a very skillful "cross-ruff" between the two throughout
Ulysses. Symbolically, Stephen and Bloom do make
several gestures which point toward a recognition of
that common humanity of which the reader is so intensely and ironically aware. As a sign of hospitality,
the older man offers his guest a "collation," a theologi-
cal term meaning a light meal which may be taken
on fast days. Together they drink "in jocoserious silence
Epps's massproduct, the creature cocoa" (677). Nearly
every commentator on *Ithaca* has dealt with that line.
William York Tindall's treatment of it is representative:
" 'Massproduct,' the key word, means three things: the
cocoa is mass-produced for the trade; as the product
of a symbolic Mass, it is the sacrament; and it suggests
the masses for whom it is produced. The drinking of
this cocoa, Stephen's communion with man, is the cli-

max of the hunt for the father."[15] Interpretations of this sort, which read so much into a phrase, may seem strained, but Joyce has in fact prepared for this particular epiphany from the point, in *Eumaeus*, where Stephen refuses to drink the coffee Bloom has bought for him. Even on the realistic plane, Bloom's minor triumph has its effect; after drinking the cocoa, Stephen becomes noticeably more open and genial. But in the end, of course, the "functions" of existence are indeed separate, and each man must cope with them alone, the indifferent stars offering no solace. As they part, the bells of St. George's remind them of death. Bloom thinks of Paddy Dignam and Stephen of his mother.

Bouvard and Pécuchet, on the other hand, find their friendship for each other the one thing in life, except for Bouvard's fortune, that comes easily. Like the inheritance, it is virtually a *donnée* of the novel, and yet one cannot simply take it for granted. After each of their disappointments, the *deux bonshommes* console each other and embrace tenderly. When one recalls the importance Flaubert attached to his own friendships, he can appreciate the covert sympathy the artist felt for his characters.[16]

Bouvard and Pécuchet's relationship, which begins with a chance encounter on the Boulevard Bourdon, has as its foundation the similiarity of their backgrounds and interests. Both are forty-seven when they meet, single, *petits bourgeois*, and tired of their jobs and of living in Paris:

[15] *James Joyce: His Way of Interpreting the Modern World* (New York, 1950), p. 29. See also Sultan's discussion (pp. 388-389) of the implications, symbolic and naturalistic, of the cocoa-drinking.

[16] Cf. Benjamin F. Bart, *Flaubert* (Syracuse, 1967), pp. 589-590.

"Ils dénigrèrent le corps des ponts et chaussées, la régie des tabacs, le commerce, les théâtres, notre marine et tout le genre humain, comme des gens qui ont subi de grands déboires. Chacun en écoutant l'autre retrouvait des parties de lui-même oubliées. . . .

"Ensuite, ils glorifièrent les avantages des sciences: que de choses à connaître, que de recherches . . . si on avait le temps! Hélas! le gagne-pain l'absorbait; et ils levèrent les bras d'étonnement, ils faillirent s'embrasser par-dessus la table en découvrant qu'ils étaient tous les deux copistes, Bouvard dans une maison de commerce, Pécuchet au ministère de la Marine; ce qui ne l'empêchait pas de consacrer, chaque soir, quelques moments à l'étude." (4-5)[17]

In the rather crude scientific curiosity they oppose to the monotony of their workaday lives, the two copyists very much resemble Bloom, who believes that "intellectual stimulation as such was . . . from time to time a firstrate tonic for the mind" (646). Bloom, an advertising canvasser who on occasion describes himself as an "author-journalist," finds a good portion of his cerebral aliment in the newspapers: "give us this day our press" (647). Bouvard and Pécuchet would have little chance of progressing beyond the point of wanting to know the exact number of volumes in the

[17] "They ran down the municipal services, the tobacco monopoly, business, the theatre, the navy, and the entire human race, like men who have suffered deep disappointments. Each, as he listened to the other, discovered forgotten corners in himself. . . . Next they celebrated the advantages of science: how many facts there were to be learnt, how much to go into—if only one had the time! Alas, their daily bread occupied them; and they raised their arms in astonishment, nearly embraced over the table, on discovering that they were both copying-clerks, Bouvard in a business house, Pécuchet at the Admiralty; which did not, however, prevent him from devoting a few minutes each evening to study" (19-20).

grande bibliothèque were it not for the accident of Bouvard's becoming his "uncle's" heir. His coming into this unexpected wealth frees the two friends to devote full time to the mock-scholarly pursuits which take up most of the novel. The difference this development makes in their intellectual lives vis-à-vis Joyce's hero's is significant, as Lionel Trilling points out:

"To Bloom, ideas are the furniture or landscape of his mind, while to Bouvard and Pécuchet they exist . . . as characters in the actual world. Bloom's ideas are notions; they are bits and pieces of fact and approximations and adumbrations of thought pieced together from newspapers and books carelessly read; Bloom means to look them up and get them straight but he never does. They are subordinate to his emotions, to which they lend substance and colour. . . . But Bouvard and Pécuchet are committed to ideas and confront them fully. They amass books and study them. Ideas are life and death to them."[18]

To say that Bouvard and Pécuchet confront ideas fully is perhaps to view their case too charitably. Certainly they pursue their studies singlemindedly; indeed, the obsessional character of their endeavors contributes to the comic effect of the novel. But part of its humor stems also from the brevity of their preoccupations, from the speed with which they run through so many areas of learning. Their ludicrous ineptitude is largely a reflection of their inability to submit themselves to any one discipline in a manner rigorous enough to enable them to master it.

Obviously it was necessary for Flaubert to create some differences between his protagonists, if only for the sake of generating sufficient dialectical tension to

[18] *The Opposing Self* (New York, 1955), p. 178.

account for their movement from one set of ideas to another (although, as in *Ithaca*, very little attention is given to effecting smooth transitions). He draws the distinctions in broad strokes: Bouvard is fair, corpulent, and sanguine, whereas Pécuchet is dark, hatchet-faced, and melancholic. These divergences are nowhere more evident than in the author's synopsis for the unwritten conclusion of the book:[19]

> Pécuchet voit l'avenir de l'Humanité en noir:
> L'homme moderne est amoindri et devenu une machine. . . .
> Barbarie par l'excès de l'individualisme et le délire de la science. . . . Si les convulsions qui existent depuis 89 continuent, sans fin entre deux issues, ces oscillations nous emporteront par leurs propres forces. Il n'y aura plus d'idéal, de religion, de moralité.
> L'Amérique aura conquis la terre.
> Avenir de la littérature.
> Pignouflisme universel. Tout ne sera plus qu'une ribote d'ouvriers.
> Fin du monde par la cessation du calorique.
> Bouvard voit l'avenir de l'Humanité en beau.
> L'Homme moderne est en progrès.
> L'Europe sera régénérée par l'Asie. La loi his-

[19] Any discussion of *Bouvard et Pécuchet* must bear in mind its unfinished state. Many critics believe that Flaubert's intentions, especially his attitude toward the main characters, underwent a change in the course of the book's composition, and that the resultant inconsistencies would probably have been eliminated had there been another draft. D. L. Demorest, *A travers les plans, manuscrits, et dossiers de "Bouvard et Pécuchet"* (Paris, 1931), Chapter v, takes exception to this view, supporting his argument with extensive references to the source material of the novel.

torique étant que la civilisation aille d'Orient en Occident. . . .

Avenir de la littérature (contre-partie de littérature industrielle). Sciences futures.–Régler la force magnétique.

Paris deviendra un jardin d'hiver;–espaliers à fruits sur le boulevard. La Seine filtrée et chaude. . . .

Disparition du mal par la disparition du besoin. La philosophie sera une religion.

Communion de tous les peuples. Fêtes publiques.

On ira dans les astres,–et quand la terre sera usée, l'Humanité déménagera vers les étoiles. (392-393)[20]

[20] "Pécuchet sees the future of Humanity in dark colours.

"Modern man has been whittled down and become a machine. . . .

"Barbarity through excess of individualism and the extravagance of science. . . . If the convulsions which have been going on since '89 continue, endlessly between two issues, these oscillations will sweep us away by their own force. There will no longer be ideals, religion, morality.

"America will have conquered the earth.

"Future of literature.

"Universal vulgarity. All will be a workmen's orgy.

"End of the world through cessation of heat.

"Bouvard sees the future of Humanity in a cheerful light. Modern man is evolving.

"Europe will be regenerated by Asia. The historical law being that civilisation goes from East to West. . . .

"Future of literature (opposite of industrial literature). New sciences.–Control of magnetic force.

"Paris will become a winter garden; fruit espaliers on the boulevard. The Seine filtered and warm. . . .

"Disappearance of evil with the disappearance of want. Philosophy will be a religion.

"Alliance of all nations. Public festivals.

"People will visit other earths—and when this globe is used up, Humanity will migrate to the stars" (345-346).

Pécuchet's outlook parodies the philosophical and political pessimism commonly associated with literary intellectuals of the post-Romantic era, including Flaubert himself. It is more difficult for present-day readers to imagine that Bouvard's confident positivism had its serious proponents, as it in fact did among the numerous followers of Auguste Comte. His scientism and flights of facile optimism still appeal, of course, to many ordinary men and retain a place in the rhetoric of more than a few successful politicians. Leopold Bloom embraces both viewpoints at various times, although in *Ithaca*, at the end of a long day, he inclines toward disillusionment. In any case, the texture of Flaubert's prose in these notes clearly anticipates the style Joyce employs to render Bloom's mental life. "Joyce got a long way beyond Flaubert," comments Kenner, "but Flaubert's systematic incongruities remained his Archimedean fulcrum for altering the perspective of thought and feeling from phrase to phrase."[21] The correspondence is evident at many points in *Bouvard et Pécuchet* and *Ulysses*, but the blueprint for the ending of the former work and the *Ithaca* episode bring it into sharpest focus.

Pécuchet's associative leap from his vision of a working-class orgy to the "fin du monde par la cessation du calorique," from social decay to universal entropy, is eminently Bloomesque. Earlier in the novel, the *deux bonshommes* have scanned the heavens and reflected on the splendor and the terror of the cosmos. Flaubert's references to "grands espaces vides" (95) and "longs silences" (96) recall Pascal's celebrated *pensée* (iii.206), which provides an ironic backdrop for his protagonists' musings. As they speculate on the

[21] *Dublin's Joyce* (Boston, 1962), pp. 204-205.

probable character of inhabitants of other planets, their
thoughts are interrupted:

> Quelques étoiles filantes glissèrent tout à coup,
> décrivant sur le ciel comme la parabole d'une mon-
> strueuse fusée.
> —Tiens, dit Bouvard, voilà des mondes qui dis-
> paraissent.
> Pécuchet reprit:
> —Si le nôtre, à son tour, faisait la cabriole, les
> citoyens des étoiles ne seraient pas plus émus que
> nous ne le sommes maintenant. De pareilles idées
> vous renfoncent l'orgueil. (96-97)[22]

And they go on to wonder at the meaning of creation
or whether indeed it has any meaning. Finally, Bouvard, overwhelmed by the mystery of it all and by the
brandied coffee he has been sipping, declares that the
answer must be in Buffon and goes to bed. Their cos-
mological concerns are not, however, so easily laid to
rest; many pages later, during their metaphysical
phase, they ponder, "Puisque des étoiles peuvent avoir
disparu quand leur éclat nous arrive, nous admirons,
peut-être, des choses qui n'existent pas" (281-282).[23]
Their initial encounter with the stars prompts the
two friends to undertake a series of quasi-scientific in-
vestigations. Quickly tiring of such pedestrian subjects

[22] "Some shooting stars fell suddenly, describing what seemed
the parabola of a gigantic rocket on the sky.
"'Look!' said Bouvard, 'there are worlds vanishing.'
"Pécuchet replied:
"'If ours in its turn made a plunge, the citizens of the stars
would not be more moved than we are now. Such ideas check
one's pride'" (94).

[23] "Since stars may have perished by the time their beams
reach us, we are perhaps admiring things that do not exist"
(250).

as the nature of minerals, they turn to the *Harmonies* of Bernardin de Saint-Pierre, a philosophical treatise "qui découvre dans la nature des intentions vertueuses et la considère comme une espèce de saint Vincent de Paul toujours occupé à répandre des bienfaits" (98).[24] For the moment at least, they crave some principle of integration for the welter of facts that confronts them. The same impulse underlies their experiments with various mnemonic systems. They take their own house as a base, allowing each part to stand for a different fact, until before long the house, the garden, and the surrounding countryside have no meaning except as aids to recollection: "le monde devenait symbole" (152).[25]

The need to stack immense quantities of mental lumber has Bloom too worrying about "defective mnemotechnic" (689). Astronomy is the science that particularly appeals to him, Frank Budgen thinks, "because its real vagueness and its air of precision provoke his imagination and because the vast times and spaces with which it deals flatter his pessimism by making him feel small. . . . He seems to have an innate knowledge of the second law of thermodynamics. His universe is running down."[26] As Bloom and Stephen step into the former's backyard, they are greeted by "the heaventree of stars hung with humid nightblue fruit" (698). "Heaventree" is Stephen's idiom, but the meditation which follows is Bloom's. He contemplates the "parallactic drift of socalled fixed stars, in reality evermoving from immeasurably remote eons to infinitely

[24] "They were filled with that philosophy which discovers virtuous intentions in Nature and looks on her as a kind of Saint Vincent de Paul, always busy scattering bounties" (95).
[25] "The world became a symbol" (140).
[26] *James Joyce and the Making of "Ulysses,"* p. 277.

remote futures in comparison with which the years, threescore and ten, of allotted human life formed a parenthesis of infinitesimal brevity" (698). What interests him, then, are the analogies that can be drawn between macro- and microcosm; his astronomy represents a form, however attenuated, of the intellectual hierarchy of scholasticism, and it is not surprising that he augments its humane relevance with a dash of astrology when it suits his purpose. Perhaps it is inevitable that, with Joyce as his artistic sire, Bloom should have in him a trace of the same Jesuit strain that runs so strongly through Stephen. Like Bouvard and Pécuchet, Bloom considers the matter of life on other planets, but with a curious twist: he is concerned with "the possible social and moral redemption of said race by a redeemer" (699). Even an "apogean" humanity, he decides, "would probably there as here remain inalterably and inalienably attached to vanities, to vanities of vanities and all that is vanity" (700).

The Preacher's skepticism prevails as Bloom, viewing the constellations, concludes: "That it was not a heaventree, not a heavengrot, not a heavenbeast, not a heavenman. That it was a Utopia, there being no known method from the known to the unknown . . . a past which possibly had ceased to exist as a present before its future spectators had entered actual present existence" (701). As Stephen takes leave of this Ecclesiastes of Eccles Street, the two of them see a celestial sign, a star which shoots from the Lyre to Leo, a symbolic indication that even in his departure the young poet may be moving toward the maturity Leopold represents—a maturity that opposes human warmth to the cold indifference of the stars. Bloom's view of man's situation in the universe permits him to live with a certain cheerfulness; he is indeed the "victim predestined" (692), but he is also a "conscious reactor against the void" (734), and the latter attribute enables him to find various satisfactions en route to the ineluctable tragic consummation. And among these satisfactions is, in all its ambivalence, his marriage.

At one point in *Bouvard et Pécuchet*, the heroes devote themselves to hunting for phallic and vaginal symbols. The latter they interpret in the following manner:

"Que signifiaient les tumulus?

"Plusieurs contiennent des squelettes ayant la position du foetus dans la sein de sa mère. Cela veut dire que le tombeau était pour eux comme une seconde gestation les préparant à une autre vie. Donc le tumulus symbolise l'organe femelle, comme la pierre levée est l'organe mâle." (141)[27]

Bloom, however, has no need to engage in dialectic to uncover a means to his regeneration. He knows Molly lies waiting "in the attitude of Gea-Tellus, fulfilled, recumbent, big with seed" (737). Her husband, in turn, assumes a foetal posture, becoming "the childman weary, the manchild in the womb" (737). In such manner he renews himself and prepares to be reborn into a new version of the old diurnal round. So far as Bloom himself is concerned, we have reached the end of *Ulysses*. Only Molly's coda remains. Thus the structure of the novel prefigures the circularity of *Finnegans Wake*, which begins in the middle of the same sentence with which it concludes.

[27] "What does a tumulus signify?"
"Some contain skeletons placed like the foetus in the mother's womb. This means that the tomb was, as it were, a second gestation, to prepare them for another life. Thus the tumulus signifies the female, as the upright stone is the male organ" (130).

Flaubert evidently intended *Bouvard et Pécuchet* to trace a comparable cyclical pattern. His working notes reveal that, at the close of the book, when everything the two friends have undertaken has turned to ashes in their mouths, they were to have sought refuge in their former vocation: *"Copier comme autrefois"* (395).[28] Perhaps, as with Camus' Sisyphus and Bloom asleep beside his wife, one must imagine the two clerks happy.

[28] *"To copy as in the old days"* (347).

An artist must be in his work like God
in creation, invisible and all-powerful;
he should be everywhere felt, but nowhere
seen.

—FLAUBERT,
Letter to Mlle Leroyer de Chantepie

The artist, like the God of the creation,
remains within or behind or beyond or
above his handiwork, invisible, refined
out of existence, indifferent, paring his
fingernails.

—*A Portrait of the Artist*

It is our task to imprint this
provisional, perishable earth so
deeply, so patiently and passionately
in ourselves that its reality shall
arise in us again "invisibly."

—RILKE, Letter to Witold von Hulewicz

CHAPTER VIII

INVISIBLE NOVELISTS

THE CORE OF THE AFFINITY

AND ITS LIMITS

In the opening years of this century, when Joyce was searching for masters who could help him learn to write fiction, he found his own country a wasteland. "A nation which never advanced so far as a miracle-play," he scornfully asserted, "affords no literary model to the artist, and he must look abroad."[1] Beginning his investigation across the Irish Channel, Joyce determined that the British tradition was a shambles. Even the contemporary English novelist whose philosophical acuity he most respected, George Meredith, he declared "plainly lacking in that fluid quality, the lyrical impulse," he considered indispensable. Neither, he felt, did Meredith have "the instinct of the epical artist."[2] His estrangement from English and Irish literary circles made him, in effect, an expatriate before he ever left Dublin.

One can readily understand, then, why Joyce was attracted to Ibsen, who spent most of his career seek-

---

[1] *The Critical Writings of James Joyce*, ed. Ellsworth Mason and Richard Ellmann (New York, 1959), p. 70.
[2] *Ibid.*, p. 89.

ing refuge from the provincialism of Norway.[3] The bond between the two writers goes well beyond their refusal to yield to the conventions of their native cultures and their preoccupation with the question of exile, for both felt a need to represent realistically the common life of the societies they rejected and to redeem that life through the formal perfection of their art. Joyce praised the Norwegian master's plays for just those qualities he aspired to in his own writing: "Ibsen treats . . . all things . . . with large insight, artistic restraint, and sympathy. He sees [life] steadily and whole, as from a great height, with perfect vision and an angelic dispassionateness, with the sight of one who may look on the sun with open eyes."[4] The disparity between this image of seraphic disinterestedness and Stephen Dedalus' comparison of the artist to God in *A Portrait* is crucial and a question we shall consider in some detail subsequently. For the moment it is enough to observe that if Flaubert's Saint Antoine sees the aspect of Christ in the sun's disc and Joyce's Bloom that of Sweny the druggist, their perceptions are not so far apart as they seem. As the Stephen of *Ulysses* remarks, God is "all in all in all of us,"[5] and we may hear His voice in a cry from the street.

Joyce learned Dano-Norwegian in order to read Ibsen in the original and acquired, as a dividend, access to the works of Jens Peter Jacobsen, whose novel *Niels Lyhne* extends Ibsen's critique of illusion. Jacobsen's hero struggles toward a stoic acceptance of life, however dreary and bitter, as it is. Niels's complex attachment to a mother who shares Emma Bovary's addiction

[3] See B. J. Tysdahl, *Joyce and Ibsen* (Oslo and New York, 1968), pp. 9-46.

[4] *Critical Writings*, p. 65.

[5] *Ulysses* (New York: Modern Library, 1961), p. 212.

to dreams renders this endeavor nearly impossible. He idealizes several of the women in his life, as Frédéric Moreau does Mme Arnoux, making of them inaccessible objects before whom he abjectly and idolatrously effaces himself. When he does become involved in a full-blooded liaison with Fennimore Refstrup, the wife of his best friend, it results in an agony of remorse that anticipates Stephen's in Chapter III of the *Portrait* and, as in Stephen's case, it is exacerbated by the tension between faith and doubt. Niels resembles both Frédéric and Stephen in the difficulty he encounters when he tries to fulfill himself in the poetic vocation he has, significantly enough, consecrated to his mother. Jacobsen, himself an anguished pursuer of the *mot juste*, deals more generously with the beleaguered Niels than either Flaubert or Joyce do with their young men.

French and Italian were the languages in which Joyce specialized at University College. Among the contemporary writers that command of the latter tongue made available to him, the most significant was surely Gabriele D'Annunzio, and behind the Tuscan was, once more, Flaubert. Jacobsen's Apollonian protagonist has as his ideal an "imageless view of life"[6] while the Dionysian hero of *Il Fuoco* maintains that "one cannot think if not in images" and the "secret analogies" that bind them.[7] Indeed D'Annunzio repeatedly apostrophizes Stelio Effrena as *l'Imaginifico*, the Image-maker; moreover, his novel, the opening section of which is entitled "The Epiphany of the Flame," is nothing if not an opulent brocade of symbols. His symbols partake, as Coleridge has it, of the things they render intelligi-

---

[6] *Niels Lyhne*, trans. H. A. Larsen (Garden City, N.Y., and Toronto, 1921), p. 266.

[7] *The Flame of Life*, trans. Kassandra Vivaria [pseud.] (New York, 1900), pp. 9, 26.

ble; words are "of almost carnal essence . . . those living substantial words with which he had often touched
women as if with caressing and inviting fingers."[8] Like
Frédéric and Niels, Stelio imaginatively transfigures
women—not so they will become unattainable but
rather that he may possess them more fully, may incarnate his fictions in them. He shares Stephen's con-
viction that in the "womb of the imagination" the word
can be made flesh, although he does not insist that the
womb be virginal. The richly metaphorical and musical
prose of *Il Fuoco* as well as its almost transitionless
narrative technique owe a great deal to the "divin Flaubert,"[9] especially to the Flaubert of *La Tentation de
saint Antoine* and *Salammbô*, and of course they point
the way to *A Portrait of the Artist*.

Joyce knew very well the line of development in
which his fiction would take its place. Almost two years
before he began work on his *Künstlerroman*, he remarked of his compatriot George Moore that he was
"really struggling in the backwash of a tide that has
advanced from Flaubert through Jakobsen to D'Annunzio: for two entire eras lie between *Madame Bovary*
and *Il Fuoco*."[10] Moore found the Irish literary scene as
barren as Joyce did and reacted by going to school with
the French writers—at the expense of whatever originality he might once have possessed. Moore's models were,
from Joyce's standpoint, unsuitable: Huysmans' work

[8] *Ibid.*, p. 56. *Tutte le opere* (Rome, 1927), IV, 66: ". . .
parole dall'aspetto quasi càrneo, quelle vive sostanziali parole
con cui egli sapeva toccare le donne come con dita carezzevoli
e incitatrici."

[9] Gabriele D'Annunzio, *Correspondance à Hérelle*, trans. Guy
Tosi (Paris, 1946), p. 114: "Il faut rendre plus musicales certaines cadences, certaines chutes de phrases comme dirait votre
divin Flaubert."

[10] *Critical Writings*, p. 71.

had, he felt, grown "more formless and more obviously comedian,"[11] and Zola's art, though it drew strength from its representation of ordinary life, dissipated much of that power in the crudeness of the language with which the author of *L'Assommoir* bludgeoned his readers.

The master Joyce required had to unite the naturalists' stress on fundamental human concerns with the symbolists' attention to the rich possibilities of form. In Flaubert, writing just before the two movements parted ways, he found his man. Nathalie Sarraute, discussing Flaubert's role as a precursor of the *nouveau roman*, indicates at the same time one of the major reasons Joyce was attracted to him: "To see through appearances, to discover a new fictional substance and give it life, Flaubert chose the right position, at once remote and yet entirely committed."[12] One misses the point of the analogy between the artist and God if he fails to see that the artificer is not absent from his creation, only invisible. His devotion to the rendering of life can, as Flaubert suggests, be felt in every word. Rather than the "indifference" of which Stephen speaks, one finds in superior art a scrupulous balance of sympathy and detachment.

The novelists' overstatement of the doctrine of impassivity has been responsible for a great deal of confusion. Flaubert replied to a query as to how much of himself he put into *Madame Bovary* by claiming that "it is a *totally fictitious* story; it contains none of my feelings and no details from my own life. The illusion of truth (if there is one) comes, on the contrary, from the book's impersonality. It is one of my principles that

11 *Ibid.*, p. 123.
12 "Flaubert," *Partisan Review* (spring 1966), XXXIII, 202.

a writer should not be his own theme."[13] Yet it is evident that with varying measures of sympathy and irony he identifies with Emma and many of his other characters. Tradition credits him with having acknowledged, "Madame Bovary, c'est moi!" How can one resolve this apparent contradiction? The answer lies, I think, in Keats's concept of negative capability—the artist's imaginative projection of himself into the world he is forging. Consider the following account Flaubert gives of his work on part II, Chapter IX of *Bovary*: "It is a delicious thing to write, whether well or badly—to be no longer yourself but to move in an entire universe of your own creating. Today, for instance, man and woman, lover and beloved, I rode in a forest on an autumn afternoon under the yellow leaves, and I was also the horse, the leaves, the wind, the words my people spoke, even the red sun that made them half-shut their love-drowned eyes."[14] "Madame Bovary, c'est moi" actually means that the artist can become Emma when the occasion demands, although she cannot under any circumstances become Flaubert.

No doubt his contention that *Madame Bovary* contains none of his sentiments or experience is hyperbolic, and the claim would be even less tenable in the case of the *Education* or the *Tentation*. All the same, whatever personal elements these books embody have been objectified and universalized in the dramatic form, so that their significance for the reader is governed by the manner in which they are rendered rather than their subjective importance to the author.

The same principle obtains in Joyce's work, the auto-

[13] *The Selected Letters of Gustave Flaubert*, trans. and ed. Francis Steegmuller (New York, 1953), p. 195 (*Correspondance* [Paris: Conard, 1926-1933], IV, 164).
[14] *Selected Letters*, p. 166 (*Correspondance*, III, 405).

biographical character of his material notwithstanding. In the *Scylla and Charybdis* episode of *Ulysses*, Stephen amplifies his remarks in *A Portrait* on the artist's resemblance to God. He does so in the context of his *Hamlet* theory, the key to which is his belief that Shakespeare "found in the world without as actual what was in his world within as possible": "We walk through ourselves, meeting robbers, ghosts, giants, old men, young men, wives, widows, brothers-in-love. But always meeting ourselves. The playwright who wrote the folio of this world and wrote it badly (He gave us light first and the sun two days later), the lord of things as they are whom the most Roman of catholics call *dio boia*, hangman god, is doubtless all in all in all of us."[15] Joyce and Flaubert seek to extend Terence's dictum: nothing human—or inhuman—should be alien to the writer.

The novelists' concern with impersonality goes hand in hand with their reflections on the ontological status of the literary word—its relation to the thing it names, its position in the mind of author and reader, and the ways in which all three act on the word and are acted upon by it. It is the problem that confronts Goethe's Faust when he attempts to translate the term *Logos* in the opening phrase of St. John's Gospel. Joyce has Stephen try to resolve it by shifting his metaphor from the Incarnation, the Word become flesh, to the Assumption, the body assimilated into an ideal realm: "In woman's womb word is made flesh but in the spirit of the maker all flesh that passes becomes the word that shall not pass away."[16] (Stephen's dilemma is the perennial one of *homo duplex*, the "folio" in little; his soul has been formed in a culture whose nets it seeks to elude and finds itself fastened to a dying animal it wishes

[15] *Ulysses* (New York: Modern Library, 1961), p. 213.
[16] *Ibid.*, p. 391.

mot juste for Joyce extends, then, far beyond the matter of fidelity to fact. Convincing representation and incisive analysis demand the word that will express a thing "as it *always* is, in itself, in its essence, freed of all ephemeral contingencies."[19] Grounding himself in what Stephen refers to as the "ineluctable modality" of sensory experience, the artist reads the "signature" of each thing, the word that captures its *quidditas* or whatness.[20] Settling on the exact word entails not only an etymologically precise understanding of it but also the assurance that it has attained an integral relation, cognitively and musically, to the total context.[21] Even in *Bouvard et Pécuchet* and *Ithaca* where the style appears most atomistic, the very dislocations function as parts of a structural "rhythm," an all-encompassing word. In this commitment to the word in its broadest meaning, "the universal creative word which is all words,"[22] lies the heart of the affinity between the two novelists.

Important as the doctrines Flaubert enunciated in his letters are to a comprehension of Joyce's art, it need hardly be pointed out that the latter learned far more from the example of the French master's fiction. There would be little value, however, in a summary rehearsal of connections that have required six chapters to explore and that can be properly understood only with detailed reference to the novels. But this does seem an appropriate place to define the limits of Joyce's sym-

19 *Selected Letters*, p. 138 (*Correspondance*, II, 462).

20 Cf. *Ulysses*, p. 37; *Portrait*, pp. 212-213.

21 Cf. Haskell M. Block, "Theory of Language in Flaubert and Joyce," *Revue de littérature comparée*, XXXV (1961), 199-200.

22 Northrop Frye, *Anatomy of Criticism* (Princeton Univ. Press, 1957), p. 125.

pathy with Flaubert and to suggest a few of the more significant respects in which he goes beyond precedents set by the Frenchman.

Several of the narrative techniques Joyce gleaned from Flaubert served as the bases for new methods of rendering subjective experience. The Frenchman's desire "to give to psychological analysis the swiftness, clarity, and impetus of a strictly dramatic narrative"[23] led to his discovery of free indirect discourse, which gives the reader access to characters' thoughts and at the same time permits the author to distance himself from the story. Joyce naturalized the *style indirect libre* as a vehicle for English fiction in *Dubliners* and the *Portrait*, then went a step further and developed the interior monologue, a mode that enables the artist to probe more deeply into the psyche and to conceal himself still more effectively behind his handiwork. There is nothing in Flaubert's books equivalent to the spiral of Bloom's sensations as he drops off to sleep at the end of *Ithaca* or to the flux of Molly's night-thoughts in *Penelope*. The drama of the unconscious in the *Tentation* closely approximates that of *Circe*, but, as we have seen, it lacks the coherence that Joyce gains by anchoring the events of that episode elsewhere in his narrative, providing them with naturalistic underpinnings.

The *Tentation* is the only Flaubert novel that even begins to approach the dream psychology of *Finnegans Wake*, which portrays history as a seamless conjunction of the nightmarish and the comic. Recalling Joyce's admiration for Flaubert and Defoe, James Atherton asserts that "there are too many real—or rather, fully realized—characters taking part in the action for the

---

[23] *Selected Letters*, p. 139 (*Correspondance*, II, 469).

[*Wake*] to be anything except a novel of the naturalistic type."[24] How different the "realism" of Joyce's last book is, however, from the naturalists' depiction of representative slices of life. *Finnegans Wake* thrusts toward all-inclusiveness and in doing so sacrifices the controlling devices, the selective focus, that determine the pattern of most naturalistic narratives. The *Wake* does have affinities with the encyclopedic exhaustiveness and circular design of *Bouvard et Pécuchet* (these aspects of the two works reflect their authors' aversion to the procrustean manipulation of reality into conventional plots and factitious endings); however, Joyce's novel is markedly denser in texture and more elaborate in structure than Flaubert's, and it relies on symbolist techniques to a degree unparalleled in fiction. We find in the *Wake* an abandonment of consecutive narration, a telescoping of time, and a cubistic rearrangement of perspectives that extend far beyond any of Flaubert's experiments with spatial or contrapuntal form. The "symphonic" method of the *Comices agricoles* remotely prefigures these developments, but if we are looking for models of orchestration on a scale approaching that of the *Wake* we will discover a much more pertinent one in Mallarmé's *Un Coup de dés*.[25] Joyce's dissolution of conventional narrative time entails a perception of simultaneity on the reader's part that allows him, like God and the artist, to see the cosmos *sub specie aeternitatis*, although the quantity of knowledge he must accumulate beforehand may have him chewing rather than paring his fingernails.

Ironically, Joyce chose the novel in which he realizes his holistic aspirations most fully to relinquish the

[24] *The Books at the Wake* (New York, 1960), p. 13.
[25] Cf. David Hayman, *Joyce et Mallarmé* (Paris, 1956), 2 vols., *passim*.

artist/God simile. The young writer's obsession with
the demands of his calling, which occupies center
stage in *A Portrait*, receives less emphasis in *Ulysses*,
which concerns itself more with the problems of a family man. This displacement extends further in *Finnegans Wake*, whose hero, Humphrey Chimpden Ear-
wicker, represents all fathers. His son Shem, who often
seems a caricature of the poet, recasts Stephen's observations on the artist's meeting himself in the world:
"The first till last alshemist wrote over every square
inch of the only foolscap available, his own body, till
by its corrosive sublimation one continuous present
tense integument slowly unfolded all marryvoising
moodmoulded cyclewheeling history (thereby, he said,
reflecting from his own individual person life unliv-
able, transaccidentated through the slow fires of consciousness into a dividual chaos, perilous, potent, common to allflesh, human only, mortal)."[26]

The novelist confesses that, having sundered himself
from the community of his birth, he has been driven
to write on "the only foolscap available," his own life.
If Shem cannot claim a link to God, even to the "hangman god" of Stephen Dedalus, he nevertheless reaffirms the faith that what his art expresses is the quin-
tessential experience of the race. For the Viconian
Joyce autobiography coincides with "cyclewheeling history" in its most significant form, myth, and of this
"dividual chaos" Joyce sought to become the pan-European Tolstoy.

Flaubert preceded him into several of the darker corners of history, but he did not find there or succeed in
fabricating "one continuous present tense integument."
For the "hermit of Croisset" the time was out of joint,

[26] *Finnegans Wake* (New York, 1958), pp. 185-186.

and the bonds between the classical and medieval past with its fierce, mysterious energy and a modern world dominated by the bourgeois seemed irreparably ruptured; his nostalgia and antipathy found expression in two largely discontinuous sets of fiction. Joyce managed to hold these elements in tension, to juxtapose and even to fuse heroic antiquity with contemporary life in a single vision.[27] He began his career with a dislike and fear of the "rabblement" as strong as Flaubert's and concluded it in *Ulysses* and the *Wake* with what Richard Ellmann has rightly termed a "justification of the commonplace. . . . Joyce's discovery, so humanistic that he would have been embarrassed to disclose it out of context, was that the ordinary is the extraordinary."[28] Those attributes "common to allflesh" make it possible to align an Achaean warrior-king and an Irish-Jewish advertising canvasser without debasing the archetype of wholeness that informs them both. Frank Budgen asked the novelist whether he meant his Dublin Odysseus to be complete in the sense of being three-dimensional or in the sense of being ideal. "He is both," said Joyce. "I see him from all sides, and therefore he is all-around in the sense of your sculptor's figure. But he is a complete man as well—a good man. At any rate, that is what I intend that he shall be."[29] For the mature artist, as for the young man celebrating Ibsen, seeing life steadily and whole entailed a marriage of the Hellenic and the Hebraic in a way that Flaubert, as an intellectual descendent of Descartes and Voltaire, could never accomplish.

[27] Ezra Pound first marked this distinction between the two novelists in "Joyce et Pécuchet," *Mercure de France*, CLVI (1922), 315.

[28] *James Joyce* (New York, 1959), p. 3.

[29] *James Joyce and the Making of "Ulysses"* (Bloomington, Ind., 1960), p. 17.

Reconciling antinomies in the Joycean manner requires an imaginative synthesis of which no man in whom skeptical and rationalist tendencies predominate is capable. Flaubert remained, at the most profound level, blocked from entering a realm that can be approached only intuitively, the sphere of the eternally mysterious female. He knew it existed and longed for admittance, as Frédéric yearned for Mme Arnoux, and along with the hero of the *Education* he found himself rendered spiritually impotent by a disposition alternately to idealize and to degrade womankind. The Queen of Sheba in his *Tentation* describes herself as "a world"—one that Flaubert, like the sado-masochistic Saint Antoine, felt ultimately compelled to reject. *Madame Bovary* offers still clearer evidence of his inability to penetrate the feminine heart to its depths. As Baudelaire shrewdly observed: "He could not keep from infusing virile blood into the veins of his creature, and because of her energy and ambition and capacity for revery, Madame Bovary remained a man. Like the armored Pallas sprung from the forehead of Zeus, this bizarre androgyne has kept all of the seductive quality of a virile spirit in a charming feminine body."[30] Nowhere is Emma less a woman than in the refusal to accept her own fecundity; she despises the child she has borne but which bears no relation to her design on the world.

That Joyce, together with Bloom, "understood or felt what a woman is"[31] one can hardly doubt. In his last two novels particularly one is struck by the intimacy of his acquaintance with that other world. Anna Livia's

[30] Charles Baudelaire, *"Madame Bovary," L'Artiste* (Oct. 18, 1857), reprinted in *Flaubert*, ed. and trans. Raymond Giraud (Englewood Cliffs, N.J., 1964), p. 92.

[31] *Ulysses*, p. 782.

affirmative force shines through the *Wake* as radiantly
as the light in Molly's window towards the end of
Ulysses, the "visible luminous sign" of woman's power
over the "effluent and refluent waters" of life.[32] Walking through experience Joyce and Flaubert encoun-
tered many selves, male and female, but the latter
never discovered that complementary self the Irish
writer and his mature protagonists found in their wives.
The satisfactions of family life aided Joyce in reaching
a genial and humane poise that Saint Polycarp, as
Flaubert with whimsical irascibility signed himself,
could never attain, and from this self-possession stems
Joyce's superior capacity for comic integration.

Midway through *Finnegans Wake* appears an adap-
tation of La Fontaine's fable of the ant and the
grasshopper. Both novelists displayed the Ondt's fastidiousness in their quest for formal perfection and the
Gracehoper's faith and sense of delight in their artistic
powers. Indeed the saturnine Flaubert seldom knew
happiness apart from the experience of writing. He
told Louise Colet: "I love my work with a love that is
frenzied and perverted, as an ascetic loves the hair
shirt that scratches his belly. Sometimes, when I am
empty, when words don't come . . . I collapse on my
couch and lie there dazed . . . blaming myself for this
demented pride which makes me pant after a chimera.
A quarter of an hour later everything changes; my
heart is pounding with joy."[33]

For Joyce, ever the Gracehoper "hoppy on akkant
of his joyicity," the pleasure one feels in a book that
renders "whatever is substantial . . . in human for-
tunes" is the true measure of its excellence.[34] Each

[32] *Ibid.*, p. 702.
[33] *Selected Letters*, pp. 131-132 (*Correspondance*, II, 394).
[34] *Finnegans Wake*, p. 414; *Critical Writings*, p. 144.

INDEX

Adams, R. M., 97n
Arabian Nights, 118-19
Arnold, Matthew, 111
art, and autobiography, 35-36, 181-83; autonomy of, vi, 11, 12; impersonality of, 36-37, 58, 77-80, 178, 181-83; religion of, vii-viii, 10-11, 14, 22, 25, 49-52, 64, 71, 183-85, 187-88, 192
Atherton, James, 186-87
Auerbach, Erich, 77-78

Balzac, Honoré de, *Le Père Goriot*, 82
Barkentin, Marjorie, 127n
Bart, B. F., 132n, 163n, 184n
Baudelaire, Charles, 54n, 190; *Le Cygne*, 83; *Les Fleurs du mal*, 80; *Les petites vieilles*, 29
Beckett, Samuel, 32; *Waiting for Godot*, 32n
Bergson, Henri, 54
Block, Haskell, vi, 185n
Bloom, Leopold, 31, 66, 75, 86-87, 92, 107-108, 110-21, 132-40, 143-49, 157-65, 168, 170-73, 178, 190
Booth, Wayne, 37n, 61
Bopp, Léon, 89
Bouilhet, Louis, 40
Bourget, Paul, 36-37
Bovary, Emma, 8, 18, 40, 43, 72-74, 76-78, 80-83, 87-92, 94, 95, 97, 99, 101-106, 108, 110-13, 115, 117, 119, 178, 182, 190
Brombert, Victor, 24n, 44, 65n
Budgen, Frank, v, 4, 99, 105, 127-28, 146, 159, 170, 189

Camus, Albert, 173
Cervantes Saavedra, Miguel de, *Don Quixote*, 34, 35n, 67, 105
Chekhov, Anton, 19
Chevalier, Ernest, 6
Coleridge, S. T., 8, 179
Colet, Louise, 4, 98

Colling, Alfred, 71n, 149
Colum, Padraic, 127n

Dante Alighieri, 65, 66
D'Annunzio, Gabriele, *Il Fuoco*, 179-80
Dedalus, Stephen, 7, 12, 38, 44-53, 58-67, 73, 75-79, 84-88, 91-92, 110, 116, 117, 126, 138, 143-49, 159-63, 170-71, 178, 179, 181, 184, 188
Defoe, Daniel, 186
Demorest, D. L., 166n
Descartes, René, 189
Du Camp, Maxime, 12
Dumas, Alexandre, *The Count of Monte Cristo*, 46-47

Eliot, T. S., 154
Ellmann, Richard, 7n, 13n, 19n, 114n, 136n, 189
epiphany, 22-25, 28-30, 39-40, 48

Feydeau, Ernest, 9
FLAUBERT, GUSTAVE, *passim*
 Bouvard et Pécuchet, vii, 18, 24, 152-57, 163-73, 185, 187
 L'Education sentimentale, 7-9, 34-48, 52-58, 60, 61, 65-67, 71-72, 148n, 179, 182, 190
 Madame Bovary, 5, 8, 12, 13, 18, 35, 70-74, 76-83, 87-92, 94-105, 108-13, 115-19, 178, 180-82, 190
 Mémoires d'un fou, 36n
 Novembre, 36n
 La Tentation de saint Antoine, vii, 99, 124-32, 139-43, 145-47, 149, 178, 180, 182, 186, 187, 190
 Trois Contes, 17-18, 22, 24, 29; *Un Coeur simple*, 17-25, 27, 29, 31, 40; *La Légende de saint Julien l'hospitalier*, vii, 16, 17, 22, 31-32
 Salammbô, vii, 35, 132n, 180

Forster, E. M., 95
Fra Angelico, 39
Frank, Joseph, 96-98
Freud, Sigmund, 44n
Frye, Northrop, 71, 185

Gautier, Théophile, 54n
Geckle, G. L., 63n
Gérard-Gailly, Emile, 42n
Gifford, Don, 26
Gilbert, Stuart, 126n, 139n
Goethe, J. W. von, *Faust*, 110,
    125-26, 183
Goldberg, S. L., 19, 52, 61, 96n,
    111, 146, 159
Gordon, Caroline, 37n

Hayman, David, 38n, 187n
Homer, *The Odyssey*, 6, 86, 107,
    117, 189
Hugo, Victor, 83
Humphrey, Robert, 78, 105n
Huysmans, J. K., 180-81

Ibsen, Henrik, 14, 177-78, 189
impersonality, artistic, *see* art,
    impersonality of
interior monologue, 78-79, 99,
    105-106, 113, 186

Jacobsen, J. P., *Niels Lyhne*, 178-
    80
James, Henry, 42, 44, 73
JOYCE, JAMES, *passim*
    Dubliners, 13, 17-19, 22, 26,
    27, 29-30, 35, 60, 186; "Araby,"
    29, 30; "Clay," 19-21, 26-29;
    "The Dead," 16, 17, 19, 23,
    29-32; "Grace," 110; "A Little
    Cloud," 60; "A Painful Case,"
    30
    Exiles, 110, 116
    Finnegans Wake, vii, 7, 11,
    13, 30, 71-72, 80, 97n, 158,
    172, 186-91
    *A Portrait of the Artist as a
    Young Man*, 13, 34-38, 44-53,
    58-67, 114, 119, 176, 178-80,
    183, 184, 186, 188
    Stephen Hero, 8, 22, 36n,
    58, 60n

Ulysses, vii, 4, 8, 12, 13, 19,
    31, 58, 61, 65, 71-73, 75, 80,
    83, 85-87, 95-99, 105, 110, 112,
    116, 119, 125-26, 128, 134,
    138, 147-49, 153-55, 158, 162,
    164-65, 168, 172, 178, 188-91;
    Circe, 98-99, 124-28, 132-40,
    143-46, 148-49, 186; *Cyclops*,
    134-35; *Eumaeus*, 163; *Hades*,
    86-87, 143; *Ithaca*, 9, 66, 116,
    152, 155, 157-63, 166, 168,
    170-73, 185, 186; *Nausicaa*,
    94, 99, 105-108, 110-15, 117-
    21; *Nestor*, 73; *Oxen of the
    Sun*, 114, 116, 117; *Penelope*,
    186; *Proteus*, 70, 72-79, 83-88,
    91-92, 117, 143; *Scylla and
    Charybdis*, 115, 138, 183;
    Telemachus, 73; *Wandering
    Rocks*, 77n, 91, 98
    Ulysses in Nighttown, 127n

Kafka, Franz, 133
Kain, Richard, 26-27
Keats, John, 65, 182
Kenner, Hugh, 37n, 46, 60, 62,
    65n, 105, 155n, 168

La Fontaine, Jean de, 191
Lapp, J. C., 91n, 98n
Levin, Harry, 24-25, 63, 126n,
    127n, 141
Litz, A. W., 10, 96n

Magalaner, Marvin, 26-27
Mallarmé, Stéphane, 81; *L'Après-
    midi d'un faune*, 84; *Un Coup
    de dés*, 187
Meredith, Burgess, 127n
Meredith, George, 177
Milton, John, "Lycidas," 86n;
    Paradise Lost, 124
Moore, George, 180
Moore, Marianne, 47
Moreau, Frédéric, 9, 38-46, 48,
    52-58, 60, 65-67, 104, 148n,
    179, 180, 190
mot juste, 4, 179, 184-85
Murray, Josephine (Mrs. Wil-
    liam), 10

naturalism, 5, 8, 19, 27, 128, 159, 162-63, 181, 184. *See also* realism

Nerval, Gérard de, 126n

Newman, J. H., Cardinal, 59

Pascal, Blaise, 152, 168

Pater, Walter, 59, 62

Pound, Ezra, 4, 17, 18, 96, 125, 126, 153-54, 189n

Proust, Marcel, 54, 96

Rabelais, François, 153

realism, 5, 22, 31, 61, 159, 162-63, 187. *See also* naturalism

religion of art, *see* art, religion of

Richard, J.-P., 37n, 38, 128n

Rilke, R. M., 176

Rimbaud, Arthur, 65

romanticism, 7-8, 40-41, 46-47, 58, 74, 102-105, 112

Sabatier, Aglaé, 54n

Sacher-Masoch, Leopold von, 136n

Sade, D. A. F., Marquis de, 132

Saint Augustine, 32

Sainte-Beuve, C. A., vi, 6

Sand, George, 82, 154, 184

Sarraute, Nathalie, 181

Schlésinger, Elisa, 42n, 54n

Scholes, Robert, 64-65

Schorer, Mark, 60

Schutte, W. M., 86n

Scott, Sir Walter, 41

Shakespeare, William, 138, 183; *Antony and Cleopatra*, 66, 140; *Hamlet*, 85-86, 115, 138, 183; *King Lear*, 118; *Love's Labour's Lost*, 121; *Measure for Measure*, 62; *Romeo and Juliet*, 94; *The Tempest*, 70, 86-87

Spencer, Philip, 5, 67

Stevens, Wallace, vii, 192

Strindberg, J. A., *A Dream Play*, 127

style indirect libre, 77-79, 83, 105, 186

Sultan, Stanley, 158, 163n

Swinburne, Algernon, 63

symbolism, 5, 8, 19, 22, 80, 81, 88-92, 96, 162-63, 181, 184, 187

Taine, H. A., vi

Terence, 183

Thorlby, Anthony, 156

Tillett, M. B., 82n, 90

Tindall, W. Y., 37n, 84n, 117, 162-63

Tolstoy, L. N., 188

Trilling, Lionel, 165

Turnell, Martin, 37n, 54

Tysdahl, B. J., 178n

Vico, Giambattista, 188

Villiers de l'Isle-Adam, Comte Auguste de, *Axël*, 20

Voltaire (F. M. Arouet), 189

Wagner, Richard, 96

Waith, E. M., 37n

Walzl, Florence, 30n

Weaver, Harriet, 13

Wilde, Oscar, 63

Wilson, Edmund, 44n

Yeats, W. B., 63n; "Who Goes with Fergus?" 84

Zola, Emile, 27, 181; *L'Assommoir*, 181